THE HISTORY OF
MUSIC

EDITED BY
HOPE LOURIE KILLCOYNE

Britannica
Educational Publishing
IN ASSOCIATION WITH

ROSEN
EDUCATIONAL SERVICES

Published in 2016 by Britannica Educational Publishing (a trademark of Ency-clopædia Britannica, Inc.) in association with The Rosen Publishing Group, Inc. 29 East 21st Street, New York, NY 10010

Distributed exclusively by Rosen Publishing.
To see additional Britannica Educational Publishing titles, go to rosenpublishing.com.

First Edition

Britannica Educational Publishing
J. E. Luebering: Director, Core Reference Group

Rosen Publishing
Hope Lourie Killcoyne: Executive Editor
Nelson Sá: Art Director
Michael Moy: Designer
Cindy Reiman: Photography Manager
Introduction and additional content by Hope Lourie Killcoyne

Library of Congress Cataloging-in-Publication Data

The history of music/edited by Hope Lourie Killcoyne.—First edition.
     pages cm.—(The Britannica guide to the visual and performing arts)
Includes bibliographical references and index.
ISBN 978-1-68048-091-7 (library bound)
1. Music—History and criticism—Juvenile literature. I. Killcoyne, Hope Lourie, editor.
ML3928.H47 2016
780.9—dc23
                                                                2015000015

Manufactured in the United States of America

Photo credits: Cover, p. i Hill Street Studios/Blend Images/Getty Images; pp. viii–ix Tim Mosenfelder/Getty Images; p. 3 IndiaPictures/Universal Images Group/Getty Images; p. 6 Omikron/Science Source/Getty Images; p. 9 © iStockphoto.com/1970s; p. 20 Bibliotheque de la Faculte de Medecine, Paris, France/Archives Charmet/Bridgeman Images; pp. 24–25 In a private collection; p. 29 Photos.com/Thinkstock; p. 35 Archiv für Kunst und Geschichte, Berlin; p. 37 Classic Vision/age fotostock/SuperStock; p. 43 Print Collector/Hulton Archive/Getty Images; pp. 54–55 Eric Vandeville/Gamma-Rapho/Getty Images; p. 70 DEA Picture Library/Getty Images; p. 73 Ewing Galloway/Classicstock/Everett Collection; pp. 78–79 Hiroyuki Ito/Hulton Archive/Getty Images; p. 89 Apic/Hulton Archive/Getty Images; p. 102 Charles Trainor/The Life Images Collection/Getty Images; p. 105 Encyclopædia Britannica, Inc.; p. 106 Courtesy of Apple; p. 109 The Israel Museum, Jerusalem, Israel/Gift of James A. de Rothschild, London/Bridgeman Images; p. 117 Rischgitz/Hulton Archive/Getty Images; p. 120 Dieter Nagl/AFP/Getty Images; p. 127 Pascal Pavani/AFP/Getty Images; p. 129 Popperfoto/Getty Images; p. 137 Bob Schatz/Hulton Archive/Getty Images; p. 139 Kevin Mazur/WireImage/Getty Images; pp. 145, 165 Michael Ochs Archives/Getty Images; p. 147 Courtesy Everett Collection; pp. 158–159 Paul Natkin/WireImage/Getty Images; pp. 168–169 CBS Photo Archive/Getty Images; p. 175 Hope Lourie Killcoyne; pp. 190–191 Frederic J. Brown/AFP/Getty Images; cover and interior pages graphic elements David M. Schrader/Shutterstock.com, E_K/Shutterstock.com, Valentin Agapov/Shutterstock.com, argus/Shutterstock.com, Iakov Filimonov/Shutterstock.com.

CONTENTS

Music is around us all the time: piped in through earphones, in the background of television programs and movies, on speakers in supermarkets and drugstores, and of course, in elevators. But what about favourite songs—that music that we take in through our ears and then into our hearts? Perhaps as a child it was "Take Me Out to the Ballgame." Then, a few years later, the popular "Take Me Out" by Franz Ferdinand, possibly followed by "Take Me to Church" by Hozier. Whatever our choices, there is a deep, devoted, and almost mystic connection we have with certain songs and musicians.

Alex Kapranos (*left*) and Bob Hardy of Franz Ferdinand perform at the Austin City Limits Music Festival in Austin, Tex., Oct. 2013.

Equally, we may feel extreme dislike for various kinds of music and cannot get to the player, out of the store, or off the elevator fast enough to stop hearing it.

We have thus established that music is everywhere to be heard. We love some of it and loathe some, too. But what is it? Commentators have spoken of "the relationship of music to the human senses and intellect," thus affirming a world of human discourse as the necessary setting for the art. A definition of music itself would take longer. As the ancient Greek philosopher Aristotle said, "It is not easy to determine the nature of music or why anyone should have a knowledge of it." Indeed, birdsong, in which male birds sing to attract a mate during breeding season or use vocalizations to denote (no pun intended) their territorial boundaries as a prophylactic defense against the incursion of other male birds, is most likely not viewed by birds themselves as an art form, though we humans may take delight in the various avian sounds and interpret it as such.

Early in the 20th century, it was regarded as commonplace to characterize a musical tone by the regularity of its vibrations; this uniformity gave it a fixed pitch and distinguished its sounds from "noise." Although that view may have been supported by traditional music, by the latter half of the 20th century, it was recognized as an unacceptable yardstick. Indeed, "noise" itself and silence became elements in composition, and random sounds were used (without prior knowledge of what they would be) by composers, such as the

American John Cage, and others in works having aleatory (chance) or impromptu features. Electronic machinery enabled some composers to create works in which the traditional role of the interpreter is abolished and to record, directly on tape or into a digital file, sounds that were formerly beyond human ability to produce, if not to imagine.

It may well be easiest to reduce music to its five basic elements: rhythm, tone, melody, harmony, and form.

RHYTHM

In its most general sense, rhythm (Greek *rhythmos*, derived from *rhein*, "to flow") is an ordered alternation of contrasting elements. The notion of rhythm also occurs in other arts (e.g., poetry, painting, sculpture, and architecture) as well as in nature (e.g., biological rhythms).

Unlike a painting or sculpture, which are compositions in space, a musical work is a composition dependent upon time. Rhythm is music's pattern in time. Whatever other elements a given piece of music may have, rhythm is the one indispensable element of all music. Rhythm can exist without melody, as in the drumbeats of humanity's earliest music, but melody cannot exist without rhythm. In music that has both harmony and melody, the rhythmic structure cannot be separated from them. As Plato observed, rhythm is "an order of movement."

Simply put, then, rhythm involves time—the duration, or length, of musical sounds. Tempo, the speed at which a piece is played, is sometimes associated with rhythm.

Essential to rhythm are pulsation, or steady beat, metre, and accent. When beats are combined in groups of two, three, or more to a measure, the result is called metre. Patterns of stress—strong and weak accents—are repeated over and over, as in the waltz rhythm ONE-two-three, ONE-two-three.

TONE

Acoustically, tone is a sound that can be recognized by its regularity of vibration. A simple tone has only one frequency, although its intensity may vary. A complex tone consists of two or more simple tones, called overtones. The tone of lowest frequency is called the fundamental; the others, overtones. A combination of harmonic tones is pleasant to hear and is therefore called a musical tone.

MELODY

Melody is the aesthetic product of a given succession of pitches in musical time, implying rhythmically ordered movement from pitch to pitch. Melody in Western music by the late 19th century was considered to be the surface of a group of harmonies. The top tone of a chord became a melody tone; chords were chosen for their colour and sense of direction relative to each other and were spaced so that a desired succession of tones lay on top. Any melody, then, had underlying chords that could be deduced. Thus, a good guitarist, analyzing mentally, can apply chords to a melody.

But melody is far older than harmony. The single line of melody was highly developed— e.g., in medieval European and Byzantine plainchant, in the melodies of the trouvères and troubadours, and in the ragas and *maqamat* (melody types) of Indian and Arab music. Combining several lines of melody at once is polyphony; varying a melody in different ways in simultaneous performance is heterophony; combining melody and chords is homophony. Melody probably derives from the inflections of the human voice. It involves pitch, or the relative highness or lowness of tone. When pitches are musically organized, they are referred to as scales.

Some types of music consist mostly of melody. Other types may be based on a motif, or recurring succession of notes—for example, the four notes at the beginning of Beethoven's Fifth Symphony. When the melody in a longer composition is repeated in various forms, this basic tune is said to constitute its theme, or subject.

HARMONY

Harmony, a feature in most Western music, is the sound of two or more notes heard simultaneously. In practice, this broad definition can also include some instances of notes sounded one after the other. If the consecutively sounded notes call to mind the notes of a familiar chord (a group of notes sounded together), the ear creates its own simultaneity in the same way that the eye perceives movement in a motion picture. In such cases the ear perceives the harmony that would result if the notes had sounded together. In a narrower sense, the harmony that characterizes Western music refers to the extensively developed system of chords and the rules that allow or forbid relations between chords.

Melody and rhythm can exist without harmony. By far the greatest part of the world's music is nonharmonic. Many highly sophisticated musical styles, such as those of India and China, consist basically of unharmonized melodic lines and their rhythmic organization. In only a few instances of folk and primitive music are simple chords specifically cultivated. Harmony in the Western sense is a comparatively recent invention having a rather limited geographic spread. It arose less than a millennium ago in the music of western Europe and is embraced today only in those musical cultures that trace their origins to that area.

To summarize, harmony concerns the building of chords—tones played together— derived from the scale on which the music is based. It also involves the order in which successions of chords accompany a melody.

An example of the effective use of harmony is the second movement of Beethoven's Seventh Symphony. The initial melody is a monotone tune, or one with almost no variation, but the shifting harmony adds colour, tension, and release to the composition.

FORM

Form results from the way in which rhythm, melody, and harmony are put together. Good music has unity to satisfy a listener's ear and variety to maintain interest.

One of the simplest forms of music is produced by varying and repeating the melody. For example, "Twinkle, Twinkle, Little Star" states a tune, varies it, and then restates it. This formula, often referred to as A-B-A, is the simple ternary, or three-section, form—sometimes called "song" form. A simple binary form would be A-B. A more extended form might be A-B-A-C-A—the second rondo form. A current dance tune is frequently A-A-B-A, and a blues song is A-A-B.

So that is an account of music at its elemental level. But it is, of course, an art— one concerned with combining vocal or instrumental sounds for beauty of form or emotional expression, usually according to cultural standards of rhythm, melody, and, in most Western music, harmony. Both the simple folk song and the complex electronic composition belong to the same activity, music. Both are humanly engineered; both are conceptual and auditory, and these factors have been present in music of all styles and in all periods of history throughout the world. Music is an art that, in one guise or another, permeates every human society. Modern music is heard in a bewildering profusion of styles, many of them contemporary, others engendered in past eras. Music is a protean art; it lends itself easily to alliances with words, as in song, and with physical movement, as in dance. Throughout history, music has been an important adjunct to ritual and drama and has been credited with the capacity to reflect and influence human emotion. Popular culture has consistently exploited these possibilities, most conspicuously today by means of radio, film, television, musical theatre, and the Internet. The implications of the uses of music as a bond among people (think Deadheads or devotees of hip-hop, opera, or Broadway musicals), as well as its use in psychotherapy, geriatric care, and advertising testify to a faith in its power to affect human behaviour. Publications and recordings have effectively internationalized music in its most significant, as well as its most trivial, manifestations. Beyond all this, the teaching of music in primary and secondary schools has now attained virtually worldwide acceptance.

But the prevalence of music is nothing new, and its human importance has often been acknowledged. What seems curious is that, despite the universality of the art, no one until recent times has argued for its necessity. The ancient Greek philosopher Democritus explicitly denied any fundamental need for music: "For it was not necessity that separated it off, but it arose from the existing superfluity." The view that music and the other arts are mere graces is still widespread, although the growth of psychological understanding of play and other symbolic activities has begun to weaken this tenacious belief.

As for how music came to rise from its elemental components into an art form—whether it is deemed to be a human "necessity" or not—is what this book, *The History of Music*, brings together. Readers will travel the river of musical time from early Indian and Chinese conceptions when music was first used as a sonic vector for religion through its development in the Middle Ages to great classical composers of the late 18th century to the music of today.

"Music expresses that which cannot be put into words and that which cannot remain silent."
—Victor Hugo

"If we look at music history closely, it is not difficult to isolate certain elements of great potency, which were to nourish the art of music for decades, if not centuries."
—George Crumb

"One good thing about music, when it hits you, you feel no pain."
—Bob Marley

CHAPTER ONE

HISTORICAL CONCEPTIONS

From historical accounts it is clear that the power to move people has always been attributed to music; its ecstatic possibilities have been recognized in all cultures and have usually been admitted in practice under particular conditions, sometimes stringent ones.

INDIA

In India, music has been put into the service of religion from earliest times; Vedic hymns stand at the beginning of the record. As the art developed over many centuries into a music of profound melodic and rhythmic intricacy, the discipline of a religious text or the guideline of a story determined the structure. In the 21st century the narrator remains central to the performance of much Indian traditional music, and the virtuosity of a skillful singer rivals that of the instrumentalists. There is very little concept of vocal or instrumental idiom in

VEDIC CHANTS: HUMANITY'S FIRST SONGS?

These religious chants from India consist of hymns from the Vedas, the ancient scriptures of Hinduism. The practice dates back at least 3,000 years and is probably the world's oldest continuous vocal tradition. The earliest collection, of Vedic texts is the Rigveda (Sanskrit for "The Knowledge of Verses"), the oldest of the sacred books of Hinduism, composed in an ancient form of Sanskrit about 1500 BCE, which contain about 1,000 hymns. These hymns, which were preserved orally before being written down in about 300 BCE, are chanted in syllabic style—a type of heightened speech with one syllable to a tone. Three levels of pitch are employed: a basic reciting tone is embellished by neighbouring tones above and below, which are used to emphasize grammatical accents in the texts. These Rigveda hymns are the basis for a later collection, the Sāmaveda ("Veda of the Chants"), the hymns of which are sung in a style that is more florid, melodic, and melismatic (one word to two or more notes) rather than

Brahmin children in India practice the Vedas.

syllabic, and the range of tones is extended to six or more.

A simple, numerical system of notation—together with an oral tradition that stresses absolute precision in text, intonation, and bodily gestures—has served to perpetuate this stable tradition and to ensure its uniformity throughout all parts of India. The Vedas are chanted today exactly as they were centuries ago.

the Western sense. The vertical dimension of chord structure—that is, the effects created by sounding tones simultaneously—is not a part of South Asian classical music; the divisions of an octave (intervals) are more numerous than in Western music, and the melodic complexity of the music goes far beyond that of its Western counterpart. Moreover, an element of improvisation is retained that is vital to the success of a performance. The spontaneous imitation carried on between an instrumentalist and narrator, against the insistent rhythmic subtleties of the drums, can be a source of the greatest excitement, which in large measure is because of the faithful adherence to the rigid rules that govern the rendition of ragas—the ancient melodic patterns of Indian music.

Traditional Indian music is divided between the Hindustani (northern) and Karnatic (southern) schools. (The Hindustani style is influenced by musical traditions of the Persian-speaking world.) Instrumental and vocal music is also quite varied and frequently played or sung in concert (usually by small ensembles). It is a popular mode of religious expression, as well as an essential accompaniment to many social festivities, including dances and the narration of poetic and other folk narratives.

The two schools diverged gradually, beginning in the 13th century, when the Islamic conquest of northern parts of India introduced highly influential Arab and Persian musical practices that then merged with Hindu traditions. (The influences from Muslim cultures played virtually no role in the development of Karnatak music.)

Northern India shares with the south the use of ragas (melodic frameworks for improvisation and composition), the rhythmic principles of tala (cyclic metric patterns sometimes of great complexity), and the practice of nonmetric, rhythmically "free" improvisation. Although vocal music plays an important role, instrumental music is more important in Hindustani music than it is in Karnatak; there are some purely instrumental forms, such as the theme with variations known as *gat*.

HINDUSTANI MUSIC

The most prominent instruments of Hindustani music are the sitar (a long-necked fretted lute with about 30 melodic, drone, and sympathetic strings), sarod (a short-necked unfretted lute with sympathetic and drone strings), *sarangi* (a bowed fiddle), *shehnai* (an oboelike wind instrument), tabla (a set of two drums played by one musician, the right-hand drum carefully tuned), and *tambura* (a large, long-necked lute with four strings, used only to play the supporting drone, a single repeated chord).

A typical Hindustani performance, which may last well over an hour, begins with a long,

Sitar player and composer Ravi Shankar introduced the music of India to Western audiences. His international fame peaked in the 1960s through performances in North America and Europe, the release of several popular recordings, and collaborations with Western classical, jazz, and rock musicians.

nonmetric improvisation (*alapa*, or *alap*) by the singer or melodic soloist, followed by *jor*, or improvisation without metric cycle but with a perceptible pulse, and eventually by the similar but faster *jhala*. Then follows the composed piece, which is performed with improvised variations—most typically *khayal* (a poetic form) in vocal music and *gat*, a short, rhythmically distinctive theme, in instrumental music. Here, the soloist is accompanied by the percussionist on tabla, and the improvisations often involve various kinds of virtuosic rhythmic competition and cooperation.

KARNATIC MUSIC

Karnatic (also spelled Carnatic) music of southern India (generally south of the city of Hyderabad in Andhra Pradesh state) evolved from ancient Hindu traditions and was relatively unaffected by the Arab and Iranian influences that, since the late 12th and early 13th centuries, as a result of the Islamic conquest of the north, have characterized the Hindustani music of northern India. In contrast to northern styles, Karnatak music is more thoroughly oriented to the voice. Even when instruments are used alone, they are played somewhat in imitation of singing, generally within a vocal range, and with embellishments that are characteristic of vocal music. Fewer instruments are used in Karnatak than in northern Indian music, and there are no exclusively instrumental forms.

The basic principles of raga (melody type, or framework for improvisation) and tala (cyclical rhythmic pattern) are the same in the south and north, but each musical tradition has its own repertoire of actual ragas and talas, and there are many stylistic differences as well. Karnatak music, with its more homogeneous Indian tradition, has evolved far more orderly and uniform systems for the classification of ragas and talas. Although improvisation plays a major role in Karnatak music, the repertory also consists of a vast number of composed pieces, particularly the *kriti* or *kirtana*, complex devotional songs by composers from the 16th through the 20th centuries, particularly the so-called "trinity" of great composers of the early 19th century: Tyagaraja, Muthuswami Dikshitar, and Syama Sastri.

To many listeners, the music of the south has a restrained and intellectual character as compared with the music of the more secular Hindustani traditions.

CHINA

Chinese music is one of the oldest and most highly developed of all known musical systems. Like the music of India, it has traditionally been an adjunct to ceremony or narrative. Confucius (551–479 BCE) assigned an important place to music in the service of a well-ordered moral universe. He saw music and government as reflecting one another and believed that only the superior man who can understand music is equipped to govern. Music, he thought, reveals character through the six emotions that it can portray: sorrow, satisfaction, joy, anger, piety, and love. According to Confucius, great music is in

氣備四時與天地鬼神日月合其德

教垂萬世繼堯舜禹湯文武作之師

Confucius

harmony with the universe, restoring order to the physical world through that harmony. Music, as a true mirror of character, makes pretense or deception impossible.

Chinese music history must be approached with a certain sense of awe. Indeed, any survey evokes the music of a varied, still-active civilization whose archaeological resources go back to 3000 BCE and whose own extensive written documents refer to countless forms of music not only in connection with folk festivals and religious events but also in the courts of hundreds of emperors and princes in dozens of provinces, dynasties, and periods. For all the richness of detail in Chinese sources, however, it is only for the last segment of Chinese music history—from the Song dynasty (960–1279 CE) to the present—that there is information about the actual music itself. Yet the historical, cultural, instrumental, and theoretical materials of earlier times are equally informative and fascinating. This mass of information can be organized into four large chronological units: (1) the formative period, from 3000 BCE through the 4th century CE, (2) the international period, from the 4th through the 9th century, (3) the national period, from the 9th through the 19th century, and (4) the "world music" period of the 20th and early 21st centuries. Our narrative provides an overview of the birth of music in China, the formative period.

A GLIMPSE OF CHINA'S FORMATIVE PERIOD

Chinese writings claim that in 2697 BCE the emperor Huangdi sent a scholar, Ling Lun, to the western mountain area to cut bamboo pipes that could emit sounds matching the call of the fenghuang, an immortal bird whose rare appearance signaled harmony in the reign of a new emperor. By imitating the sound of the bird, Huangdi made possible the creation of music properly pitched to harmonize his rulership with the universe. Even this symbolic birth of music dates far too late to aid in discovering the melodies and instrumental sounds accompanying the rituals and burials that occurred before the first historically verified dynasty, the Shang (c. 1600–1046 BCE). The sounds of music are evanescent, and before the invention of recordings they disappeared at the end of a performance. The remains of China's most ancient music are found only in those few instruments made of sturdy material. Archaeological digs have uncovered globular clay vessel flutes (*xun*), tuned stone chimes (*qing*), and bronze bells (*zhong*), and the word *gu*, for drum, is found incised on Shang oracle bones (turtle shells and ox bones used by rulers for ritual divination and sacrifice to obtain the grace of their ancestors).

The earliest surviving written records are from the next dynasty, the Zhou (1046–256 BCE).

Within the famous books of the period known as the Five Classics (*Wujing*), it is in the Liji ("Collection of Rituals") of the 6th–5th century BCE that one finds an extensive discussion of music. The *Yijing* ("Classic of Changes") is a diviner's handbook built around geometric patterns, cosmology, and magic numbers that indirectly may relate to music. The *Chunqiu* ("Spring and Autumn [Annals]"), with its records of major events, and the *Shujing* ("Classic of History"), with its mixture of documents and forgeries, contain many references to the use of music, particularly at court activities. There are occasional comments about the singing of peasant groups, which is an item that is rare even in the early historical materials of Europe. The *Shijing* ("Classic of Poetry") is of equal interest, for it consists of the texts of 305 songs that are dated from the 10th to the 7th century BCE. Their great variety of topics (love, ritual, political satire, etc.) reflect a viable vocal musical tradition quite understandable to contemporary audiences. The songs also include references to less-durable musical relics such as flutes, the mouth organ (*sheng*), and, apparently, two types of zithers (the *qin* and the *se*).

AESTHETIC PRINCIPLES AND EXTRAMUSICAL ASSOCIATIONS

Despite the controversial authenticity and dates of ancient Chinese written sources, a combined study of them produces tantalizing images of courtly parties, military parades, and folk festivals, but it does not provide a single note of music. Nevertheless, in keeping with the prehistoric traditions of China, the philosophies of sages, such as Confucius and Mencius (Mengzi; *c.* 371– *c.* 289 BCE), and the endless scientific curiosity of Chinese acousticians furnish a great deal of rather specific music theory as well as varied aesthetic principles. The straightest path to this material is found in the legendary quest of Ling Lun for bamboo pipes that replicate the song of the mythical fenghuang.

The charm of such a tale tends to cloud several interesting facts it contains. First, it is noteworthy that the goal of the search was to put music in tune with the universe. The value of bringing music and the cosmos into alignment is upheld in theory in the Yueji ("Annotations on Music") section of the *Liji* with such comments as:

> *Music is the harmony of heaven and earth while rites are the measurement of heaven and earth. Through harmony all things are made known, through measure all things are properly classified. Music comes from heaven, rites are shaped by earthly designs.*

Such cosmological ideals may be not merely ancient superstitions but actually cogent insights into the cultural function of music in human societies. Confucius, as pictured in *The Analects* written long after his death, had a similar view of music, including a concern for the choice of music and modes proper for the moral well-being of a gentleman. It is an open question as to how much performance practice followed the admonitions and theories of the scholars, but centuries later one finds numerous pictures of the wise man standing before some natural beauties while his servant follows closely behind him carrying his seven-stringed zither (*qin*) for proper use in such a proper setting.

Another point to be noted in the legend of the origin of music is that Ling Lun went to the western border area of China to find the correct bamboo. Indeed, cultures from Central and West Asia or tribal China greatly influenced the growth and change of music in imperial China. Finally, it is significant that, although the emperor in the myth was primarily concerned with locating pipes that would bring his reign into harmony with the universe, the goal was also the creation of precise, standard pitches.

TONAL SYSTEM AND ITS THEORETICAL RATIONALIZATION

Harmonic pitches produced by the division of strings were known in China. They may have been used to tune sets of bells or stone chimes, but the classical writings on music discuss a

12-tone system in relation to the blowing of bamboo pipes (*lü*). The first pipe produces a basic pitch called yellow bell (*huangzhong*). This concept is of special interest because it is the world's oldest information on a tonal system concerned with very specific pitches as well as the intervals between them. The precise number of vibrations per second that created the yellow bell pitch is open to controversy (between middle C-sharp [C♯] and the F above) because the location of this pitch could be changed by the work of new astrologers and acousticians on behalf of a new emperor, in order that his kingdom might stay in tune with the universe. The choice of the primary pitch in China had extramusical as well as practical applications, for the length of the yellow bell pipe became the standard measure (like a metre), and the number of grains of rice that would fill it were used for a weight measure. Thus, the pipe itself was often the property not of the imperial music department but of the office of weights and measurements.

EXTRAMUSICAL ASSOCIATIONS OF PITCHES WITHIN THE TONAL SYSTEM

The five core tones of Chinese scales are sometimes connected with the five elements, or *wuxing* (earth, wood, metal, fire, and water), while the 12 pitches of the tonal system are connected by some writers with the months of the year, hours of the day, or phases of the moon. The 12 tones can also be found placed in two sets of six on imperial panpipes (*paixiao*) in keeping with the yinyang principle of complementary forces (e.g., female-male) of Chinese metaphysics. Their placement is based on the generation of the pitches of each pipe by its being either four-thirds larger or two-thirds smaller than the previous one, the smaller ones being female.

CLASSIFICATION OF INSTRUMENTS

The Chinese talent for musical organization was by no means limited to pitches. Another important ancient system called the eight sounds (*ba yin*) was used to classify the many kinds of instruments played in imperial orchestras. This system was based upon the material used in the construction of the instruments, the eight being stone, earth (pottery), bamboo, metal, skin, silk, wood, and gourd. Stone chimes, vessel flutes, and tubular flutes are examples from the first three categories. The *zhong* bronze bells are obvious metal examples. Another ancient member of the metal category is a large, so-called bronze drum (*tonggu*), which is of special interest because of its widespread archaeological distribution throughout Southeast Asia. The sounds of the drum are also intriguing, as are the designs inscribed on its bronze head and the frog figurines that often grace the head's rim. Han dynasty military expeditions to the south report that bronze drums among southern peoples represented the spirit of rain and water and rumbled like bullfrogs. The possession of such bronze drums or, later, gongs was, and still is, prestigious among peoples of Southeast Asia.

Stringed instruments of ancient China belong to the silk class because their strings were never made of gut or metal but were made of twisted silk. Drums are skin instruments, whereas percussive clappers are wood. One of the most enjoyable members of the wooden family is the *yu*, a model of a crouching tiger with a serrated ridge or set of slats along its back that were scratched by a bamboo whisk in a manner recalling the various scratched gourds of Latin American dance bands. The Chinese category of gourd is reserved for one of the ancient instruments, the *sheng* mouth organ. Seventeen bamboo pipes are set in a gourd or sometimes in a wooden wind chest. Each pipe has a free metal reed at the end encased in the wind chest. Blowing through a mouth tube into the wind chest and closing a hole in a pipe with a finger will cause the reed to sound, and melodies or chord structures may be played. Many variants of this instrumental principle can be found in Southeast Asia, and it is not possible to know with assurance where this wind instrument first appeared. Western imitations of its sound are found in the reed organ and, later, in the harmonica and the accordion.

GREECE

Although music was important in the life of ancient Greece, it is not now known how that music actually sounded. Only a few notated fragments have survived, and no key exists for restoring even these. The Greeks were given to theoretical speculation about music; they had a system of notation, and they "practiced music," as Socrates himself, in a vision, had been enjoined to do. But the Greek term from which the word "music" is derived was a generic one, referring to any art or science practiced under the aegis of the Muses. Music, therefore, as distinct from gymnastics, was all-encompassing. (Much speculation, however, was clearly directed toward that more-restricted meaning with which we are familiar.) Music was virtually a department of mathematics for the philosopher Pythagoras (c. 550 BCE), who was the first musical numerologist and who laid the foundations for acoustics. In acoustics, the Greeks discovered the correspondence between the pitch of a note and the length of a string. But they did not progress to a calculation of pitch on the basis of vibrations, though an attempt was made to connect sounds with underlying motions.

Plato (428–348/347 BCE), like Confucius, looked upon music as a department of ethics. And like Confucius he was eager to regulate the use of particular modes (i.e., arrangements of notes, like scales) because of their supposed effects on people. Plato was a stern musical disciplinarian; he saw a correspondence between the character of a person and the music that represented him or her. Straightforward simplicity was best. In the *Laws*, Plato declared that rhythmic and melodic complexities were to be avoided because they led to depression and disorder. Music echoes divine harmony; rhythm and melody imitate the movements of heavenly bodies, thus delineating the music of the spheres and reflecting the moral order of the universe. Earthly music, however, is suspect; Plato distrusted its emotional power. Music must therefore be of the right sort; the sensuous qualities of certain modes are dangerous, and a strong censorship must be imposed. Music and gymnastics in the correct balance would constitute the desirable curriculum in education. Plato valued music in its ethically approved forms; his concern was primarily with the effects of music, and he therefore regarded it as a psychosociological phenomenon.

PLATON

Plato, 17th-century oil on panel portrait

Yet Plato, in treating earthly music as a shadow of the ideal, saw a symbolic significance in the art. Aristotle carried forward the concept of the art as imitation, but music could express the universal as well. His idea that works of art could contain a measure of truth in themselves—an idea voiced more explicitly by Plotinus in the 3rd century CE—gave added strength to the symbolic view. Aristotle, following Plato, thought that music has power to mold human character, but he would admit all the modes, recognizing happiness and pleasure as values to both the individual and the state. He advocated a rich musical diet. Aristotle made a distinction between those who have only theoretical knowledge and those who produce music, maintaining that persons who do not perform cannot be good judges of the performances of others.

Aristoxenus, a pupil of Aristotle, gave considerable credit to human listeners, their importance, and their powers of perception. He denigrated the dominance of mathematical and acoustical considerations. For Aristoxenus, music was emotional and fulfilled a functional role, for which both the hearing and the intellect of the listener were essential. Individual tones were to be understood in their relations to one another and in the context of larger formal units. The Epicureans and Stoics adopted a more naturalistic view of music and its function, which they accepted as an adjunct

ARISTOXENUS
FLOURISHED 4TH CENTURY BCE

Greek philosopher Aristoxenus, considered the first authority for musical theory in the Classical world, was born at Tarentum (now Taranto) in southern Italy and studied in Athens under Aristotle and Theophrastus. He was interested in ethics as well as in music and wrote much, but most of his work is lost. Apart from his musical treatises, fragments remain of his reconstruction of the old Pythagorean ethics as well as of his biographies of Pythagoras, Archytas, Socrates, and Plato. His theory that the soul is related to the body as harmony is to the parts of a musical instrument seems to follow early Pythagorean doctrine. In musical theory, Aristoxenus held that the notes of the scale should not be judged by mathematical ratio but by the ear. Some of his remaining musical treatises include *Elements of Rhythm* (first published in 1861) and parts of his *Elements of Harmonics* (first published in 1868). Fragments of his other works still exist as well, including *Die Schule des Aristoteles; Texte und Kommentar* (1945; "The School of Aristotle; Text and Commentary").

to the good life. They gave more emphasis to sensation than did Plato, but they nevertheless placed music in the service of moderation and virtue. A dissenting 3rd-century voice was that of Sextus Empiricus, who said that music was an art of tones and rhythms that meant nothing outside itself.

Ultimately, the Platonic and Aristotelian influence in musical thought was to be dominant for at least a millennium and had a great influence on the naissance of Christian music.

MUSIC IN CHRISTIANITY

Much of the Platonic-Aristotelian teaching, as restated by the Roman philosopher Boethius (c. 480–524), was well suited to the needs of the church; the conservative aspects of that philosophy, with its fear of innovation, were conducive to the maintenance of order. The role of music as accessory to words is nowhere more clearly illustrated than in the history of Christianity, where the primacy of the text has always been emphasized and sometimes, as in Roman Catholic doctrine, made an article of faith. In the varieties of plainchant, melody was used for textual illumination; the configurations of sound took their cue from the words. St. Augustine (354–430 CE), who was attracted by music and valued its utility to religion, was fearful of its

sensuous element and anxious that the melody never take precedence over the words. These had been Plato's concerns also. Still echoing the Greeks, Augustine, whose beliefs were reiterated by St. Thomas Aquinas (c. 1225–74), held the basis of music to be mathematical; music reflects celestial movement and order.

GREGORIAN CHANTS: LITURGICAL MUSIC OF THE ROMAN CATHOLIC CHURCH

Sung either alone (monophonic) or as a group (in unison), these chants are the liturgical music of Catholicism, used to accompany the text of the mass and the canonical hours, or divine office. Gregorian chant is named after St.

Boethius and Philosophy, oil on canvas, by Mattia Preti, 17th century.

Gregory I, during whose papacy (590–604) it was collected and codified. Charlemagne, king of the Franks (768–814), imposed Gregorian chant on his kingdom, where another liturgical tradition—the Gallican chant—was in common use. During the 8th and 9th centuries, a process of assimilation took place between Gallican and Gregorian chants; and it is the chant in this evolved form that has come down to the present.

The Ordinary of the mass includes those texts that remain the same for each mass. The chant of the Kyrie ranges from neumatic (patterns of one to four notes per syllable) to melismatic (unlimited notes per syllable) styles. The Gloria appeared in the 7th century. The psalmodic recitation, i.e., using psalm tones, simple formulas for the intoned reciting of psalms, of early Glorias attests to their ancient origin. Later Gloria chants are neumatic. The melodies of the Credo, accepted into the mass about the 11th century, resemble psalm tones. The Sanctus and Benedictus are probably from apostolic times. The usual Sanctus chants are neumatic. The Agnus Dei was brought into the Latin mass from the Eastern Church in the 7th century and is basically in neumatic style. The concluding Ite Missa Est and its substitute Benedicamus Domino usually use the melody of the opening Kyrie.

The Proper of the mass is composed of texts that vary for each mass in order to bring out the significance of each feast or season. The Introit is a processional chant that was originally a psalm with a refrain sung between verses. By the 9th century it had received its present form: refrain in a neumatic style—a psalm verse in psalm-tone style—refrain repeated. The Gradual, introduced in the 4th century, also developed from a refrain between psalm verses. Later it became: opening melody (chorus)—psalm verse or verses in a virtuosically embellished psalmodic structure (soloist)—opening melody (chorus), repeated in whole or in part. The Alleluia is of 4th-century Eastern origin. Its structure is somewhat like that of the Gradual. The Tract replaces the Alleluia in penitential times. This chant is a descendant of synagogue music.

The sequence flourished primarily from about the 9th century to the 16th. In its modern form the texts are sacred poems with double-line stanzas having the same accentuation and number of syllables for each two lines. The melody of the first line was repeated for the second line of the stanza, a new melody being given to the next stanza; the music is syllabic. The Offertory originally consisted of a psalm and refrain, but by the 12th century only the refrain remained. The music is quite melismatic.

Peculiar to the Offertory is repetition of text. The Communion is, like the Offertory, a processional chant. The music is neumatic in style.

MUSICAL NOTIONS OF THE PROTESTANT REFORMATION

Martin Luther (1483–1546) was a musical liberal and reformer. But the uses he envisioned for music, despite his innovations, were in the mainstream of tradition; Luther insisted that music must be simple, direct, accessible, an aid to piety. His assignment of particular qualities to a given mode is reminiscent of Plato and Confucius. John Calvin (1509–64) took a more cautious and fearful view of music than did Luther, warning against voluptuous, effeminate, or disorderly music and insisting upon the supremacy of the text.

Protestant attitudes toward the arts were ambivalent. For the most part, Reformed Protestants felt uneasy about the arts, fearing that the symbol would be confused with the reality and that the symbol would be idolized and the reality forgotten. Thus Calvin found little room for the visual arts, though Luther showed interest and was a friend of some artists of his time, including Lucas Cranach. Luther also approved of music more than did the Swiss Reformers, though most Protestants encouraged its use. Protestants cite artists such as poet John

Portrait of Martin Luther, oil on panel by Lucas Cranach, 1529; in the Uffizi, Florence

Milton, painter Rembrandt, and composer Johann Sebastian Bach to demonstrate Protestant aesthetic achievement. What can be called the Protestant "mind" or "spirit" was especially prevalent in music and literature.

17TH- AND 18TH-CENTURY WESTERN CONCEPTIONS

In reviewing the accounts of music that have characterized musical and intellectual history, it is clear that the Pythagoreans are reborn from age to age. The German astronomer Johannes Kepler (1571–1630) perpetuated, in effect, the idea of the harmony of the spheres, attempting to relate music to planetary movement. René Descartes (1596–1650), too, saw the basis of music as mathematical. He was a faithful Platonist in his prescription of temperate rhythms and simple melodies so that music would not produce imaginative, exciting, and hence immoral, effects. For another philosopher-mathematician, the German Gottfried von Leibniz (1646–1716), music reflected a universal rhythm and mirrored a reality that was fundamentally mathematical, to be experienced in the mind as a subconscious apprehension of numerical relationships.

Immanuel Kant (1724–1804) ranked music as lowest in his hierarchy of the arts.

What he distrusted most about music was its wordlessness; he considered it useful for enjoyment but negligible in the service of culture. Allied with poetry, however, it may acquire conceptual value. Georg Wilhelm Friedrich Hegel (1770–1831) also extolled the discursive faculties, saying that art, though it expresses the divine, must yield to philosophy. He acknowledged the peculiar power of music to express many nuances of the emotions. Like Kant, Hegel preferred vocal music to instrumental, deprecating wordless music as subjective and indefinite. The essence of music he held to be rhythm, which finds its counterpart in the innermost self. What is original in Hegel's view is his claim that music, unlike the other arts, has no independent existence in space, is not "objective" in that sense; the fundamental rhythm of music (again an aspect of number) is experienced within the hearer.

After the 18th century, speculations upon the intrinsic nature of music became more numerous and profound. The elements necessary for a more comprehensive theory of its function and meaning became discernible. But philosophers whose views have been summarized thus far were not speaking as philosophers of music. Music interested them in terms extrinsic to itself, in its observable effects; in its connections with dance, religious ritual, or festive rites; because of its alliance with words; or for some other extramusical consideration. The only common denominator to be found, aside from the recognition of different types of music, is the acknowledgment of its connection with the emotional life, and here, to be sure, is that problematic power of the art to move. Various extramusical preoccupations are the *raison d'être* of "contextualist" explanations of music, which are concerned with its relation to the human environment. The history of music itself is largely an account of its adjunctive function in rituals and ceremonies of all kinds—religious, military, courtly—and in musical theatre. The protean character of music that enables it to form such easy alliances with literature and drama (as in folk song, art song, opera, "background" music) and with the dance (ritual, popular entertainment, "social," ballet) appears to confirm the wide range and influence that the Greeks assigned to it.

CHAPTER TWO

THEORIES OF MUSICAL MEANING SINCE THE 19TH CENTURY

Before the 19th century, musicians themselves seldom were theorists, if theorist is defined as one who explicates meaning. Music theory, when it was something other than the exposition of a prevalent or emerging style, was likely to be a technical manual guiding vocal or instrumental performance, a set of directions for meeting current exigencies in church or theatre practice, or a missive advocating reforms. Prolific masters, such as Johann Sebastian Bach, produced not learned treatises but monuments of art.

The 19th century saw the emergence of composer-critics (Carl Maria von Weber, Robert Schumann, Hector Berlioz, Franz Liszt), versatile artists with literary proclivities who were not, to be sure, propounding comprehensive theories or systems of thought. Richard Wagner, an active theorist, presaged a new species, the composer-author. But he did little to advance music theory. He proposed a unity of music and drama (*Gesamtkunstwerk*)—a reflection of the programmatic preoccupations of 19th-century composers—but its multiplicity of musical and extramusical elements only added to the confusion of musical thought. The distinctly musical character of Wagner's genius, clearly discernible in *The Ring of the Nibelung* (*Der Ring des Nibelungen*), a set of four operas, is in no way explained by his discursive credos. Igor Stravinsky, Arnold Schoenberg, and other composer-authors of the 20th century were somewhat more successful in elucidating their techniques and aims.

THE CONCEPT OF DYNAMISM

Ideas of music as a type of symbolism owe much to two German philosophers, Arthur Schopenhauer (1788–1860) and Friedrich Nietzsche (1844–1900), who brought to the theory of music a new concept, articulated by each in different ways and in divergent terms but faithful to the same principle—dynamism. Both saw in music an art that is not "spatialized" (hence not "objective") in the way that other arts are by the very conditions of their manifestation. Music is closer to the inner

Arthur Schopenhauer, 1855

dynamism of process; there are fewer technical (and no concrete) impediments to immediate apprehension, for an entire dimension of the empirical world has been bypassed.

Schopenhauer looked upon Platonic ideas as objectifying will, but music is

> . . . by no means like the other arts, the copy of the Ideas, but the copy of the will itself. This is why the effect of music is so much more powerful and penetrating than that of the other arts, for they speak only of shadows, but it speaks of the thing itself.

In contrast to Kant he accords a special efficacy to music:

> The effect of music is stronger, quicker, more necessary and infallible. Men have practiced music in all ages without being able to account for this; content to understand it directly, they renounce all claim to an abstract conception of this direct understanding itself.

Schopenhauer acknowledged a connection between human feeling and music, which "restores to us all the emotions of our inmost nature, but entirely without reality and far removed from their pain." Music, which he is presenting an as analogue of the emotional

life, is a copy or symbol
of the will.
Nietzsche posed
an Apollonian-
Dionysian dichotomy,
the former
representing form and
rationality and the
latter drunkenness
and ecstasy. For
Nietzsche, music was
the Dionysian art par
excellence. In *The
Birth of Tragedy* from
the *Spirit of Music*,
Nietzsche anticipated
the 20th-century
discovery that symbol
making (whether in

Friedrich Nietzsche, 1888.

dreams, myth, or art) is a necessary and to
some extent even automatic human activity.
The rich suggestiveness and prescience of
his insights embraced the concept of the
symbolical analogue—the artistic function
of ordering and heightening the ingredients
of the actual world—and the polarities of
experience symbolized in the Apollonian-
Dionysian conflict itself, which Stravinsky
also explored. Nietzsche gave short shrift to
mathematical aspects of music, and like
Schopenhauer he deprecated blatantly
programmatic music that abounds in

obvious imitations of natural sounds. Discerning a power in music to create myths, he looked upon mere tone painting as the antithesis of its essential character.

Efforts of theorists to account for the universal appeal of music and to explain its effects have, since the 19th century, been various, contradictory, and highly controversial. In identifying the chief points of view that have emerged, it must be emphasized that there are no completely isolated categories, and there is usually considerable overlapping; a single spokesman, the 19th-century English psychologist Edmund Gurney (1847–88), for example, may incorporate formalist, symbolist, expressionist, and psychological elements, in varying proportions, to explain the phenomenon of music. Although some disagreements are more apparent than real because of the inherent problems of terminology and definition, diametrically opposing views are also held and tenaciously defended.

REFERENTIALISTS AND NONREFERENTIALISTS

Among those who seek and propound theories of musical meaning, the most persistent disagreement is between the referentialists (or heteronomists), who hold that music can and does refer to meanings outside itself, and the nonreferentialists (who are sometimes called formalists or absolutists), who maintain that the art is autonomous and "means itself." The Austrian critic Eduard Hanslick, in his *The Beautiful in Music* (originally in German, 1854), was a strong proponent of music as an art of intrinsic principles and ideas, yet even Hanslick, ardent formalist though he was, struggled with the problem of emotion in music. Hanslick's views have been classified as a modified heteronomous theory.

One looks in vain for an extremist of either persuasion, referentialist or nonreferentialist. Igor Stravinsky first achieved fame as a composer of ballet music, and his works throughout his career were rich in extramusical associations. It would be a comfortable simplification to ally referentialism with program music and nonreferentialism with absolute music. But the problem cannot be resolved by such a choice, if only, first of all, because extramusical referents can vary in complexity from a mere descriptive title to the convolutions of the Wagnerian leitmotif, in which a particular musical phrase is consistently associated with a particular person, place, or thing.

Referentialists do not require an explicit program, and nonreferentialists do not necessarily denigrate program music, though they make a point of distinguishing between the

EDUARD HANSLICK

This celebrated music critic and a prolific author of works on music and concert life was born September 11, 1825, in Prague, and died August 6, 1904, in Baden, near Vienna.

Hanslick studied philosophy and law in Prague, received his doctorate from the University of Vienna in 1849, and taught there from 1856, becoming a regular professor in 1870. He was music critic for the *Wiener Zeitung* and subsequently was music editor of *Die Presse* and of the *Neue Freie Presse.* An excellent pianist, Hanslick served as a juror at various exhibitions of musical instruments, and, for his accomplishments in advancing the prestige of Austrian instrument makers, he was honoured by the Austrian government.

Eduard Hanslick, 1865

Hanslick's elegant literary style gained him a wide reputation, as did his numerous controversies with other critics. His stance was conservative, and he rejected the accomplishments of Wagner and Liszt while advocating the music of Schumann and Brahms. He tended to deny the importance of emotional response to music; rather, he emphasized formalism. His rejection of the idea that music communicates feelings has occasioned attacks by later writers.

Hanslick's best known book, *Vom musikalisch-Schönen* (1854; *The Beautiful in Music*, 1891), has been published in many editions and translations.

extramusical program and the musical meaning. The American musicologist and theorist Leonard Meyer, in his *Emotion and Meaning in Music* (1956), spoke of "designative" and "embodied" meanings; he recognized both kinds in music but appeared to give equal weight to the extrinsic and intrinsic.

If there is intrinsic, or embodied, meaning, one may well ask what meaning is embodied and how it is to be apprehended. An extreme formalist would say that the acoustic pattern itself and nothing more is the sense of music; Hanslick, indeed, said this, though he did not hold consistently to the view. But most nonreferentialists regard

IGOR STRAVINSKY

One of the giants in 20th-century musical composition, the Russian-born Igor Stravinsky was both original and influential. He restored a healthy unwavering pulse essential to ballet; he was meticulous about degrees of articulation and emphasis; he created a "clean" sound, with no filling in merely for the sake of filling in; he wrote for different instrumental groupings and created a different sound in every work; he revived musical forms from the past; and he made a lasting contribution to serial, or 12-tone, music.

Igor Fyodorovich Stravinsky was born on June 17, 1882, in Oranienbaum, near St. Petersburg, Russia, the son of the leading bass at the Russian Imperial Opera. Although he was taught piano, harmony, and counterpoint as a child, his family determined that he would have a career in law, and he graduated from St. Petersburg University in 1905. He had met the composer Nikolai Rimski-Korsakov in 1902 and from 1903 to 1906 studied privately with him—mainly instrumentation and analysis. Through the influence of Rimski-Korsakov, Stravinsky's early works such as

Symphony in E Flat, Fireworks, and *Scherzo Fantastique* received performances. The ballet impresario Sergei Diaghilev heard the performances and engaged Stravinsky to orchestrate various pieces of ballet music for the 1909 season of his Ballets Russes in Paris. This began a long collaboration, which produced such major works as *The Firebird* (1910), *Petrushka* (1911), *The Rite of Spring* (1913), *Pulcinella* (1920), and *The Wedding* (1923).

In his early years with the Ballets Russes, Stravinsky spent more and more time outside Russia, and with the advent of World War I he lived in Switzerland. During these years he produced two strikingly original

Igor Stravinsky, 1920

(continued on the next page)

(continued from the previous page)

stage works—*Renard* (1916), "a burlesque in song and dance," and *The Soldier's Tale* (1918), "to be read, played, and danced."

After the war Stravinsky moved to France, where he developed subsidiary careers as a concert pianist and conductor. Invited to lecture at Harvard University in 1939, Stravinsky moved to the United States, making his home in Hollywood, California. The war years produced the *Symphony in C Major*, the summation of neoclassical principles in symphonic form, and *Symphony in Three Movements*, which combines features of the concerto with the symphony.

From 1948 to 1951 Stravinsky worked on his neoclassical opera, *The Rake's Progress*, conducting its first performance in Venice. Ill health slowed Stravinsky in his final years, and he died in New York City on April 6, 1971. He was buried in Venice on the island of San Michele.

music as, in one way or another, emotionally meaningful or expressive. Referentialists, too, find expressive content in music, though this emotional content may be extramusical (even if not explicit) in origin, according to the American theorists John Hospers in *Meaning and Truth in the Arts* (1946) and Donald Ferguson in *Music as Metaphor*

(1960). Meyer made the observation that while most referentialists are expressionists, not all expressionists are referentialists. He made the useful distinction between absolute expressionists and referential expressionists and identified his own position as "formalist-absolute expressionist." In acknowledging that music can and does express referential (designative) meanings as well as nonreferential ones, Meyer exhibited an eclectic and certainly permissive view. But he has been criticized for failing to make clear the modus operandi of this referential meaning in music.

INTUITION AND INTELLECT

Most theorists agree that music is an auditory phenomenon and that hearing is the beginning of understanding. Beyond this consensus there is little agreement. There is contention especially between proponents of intuition, such as Benedetto Croce (1866–1952), and champions of intellectual cognition, such as Hospers. Gurney was constrained to postulate a special musical faculty that need not reside exclusively either in the mind or the heart. The main problem for theorists arises from the inveterate tendency to dichotomize thought and feeling. Henri Bergson (1859–1941) broke with this tradition when he spoke for "an intellectual act of intuition." In the first half of the 20th century, a reawakened philosophical and artistic concern for the concept of organic unity revealed strong affinities among such disparate works as Gurney's *The Power of Sound* (1880), the American philosopher Susanne K. Langer's *Philosophy in a New Key* (1942) and her later works, John Dewey's classic *Art as Experience* (1934), and the American composer Roger Sessions's *The Musical Experience* (1950).

It is apparent that music is connected in some way with human emotional life, but the "how" continues to be elusive. Sessions (echoing Aristotle) stated the problem fairly:

> *No one denies that music arouses emotions, nor do most people deny that the values of music are both qualitatively and quantitatively connected with the emotions it arouses. Yet it is not easy to say just what this connection is.*

It was long fashionable to speak of the "language" of music, or of music as the "language of the emotions," but, since a precise semantics is wanting in music, the analogy breaks down. Two or more listeners may derive very different "meanings" from the same piece of music, and, since written and spoken language cannot render these musical "meanings," whatever they may be, in consistent and commonly recognizable terms, verbal explication often seems to raise more questions than it settles. Philosophical analysts who hold that all meaning is capable of rendition in language therefore pronounce music—unless it can be saved by the referentialists—without meaning, confronting thoughtful listeners, thereby, with a proposition that seems clearly to contradict (and trivialize) their own experiences. The difficulty, of course, is a semantic one and explains why some theorists have substituted such terms as "import," "significance," "pattern," or "gestalt" for "meaning." Recognizing an incompatibility between the modalities of nonverbal arts and their treatment by discursive thought, it is hardly surprising that music aestheticians have been few.

SYMBOLIST CONTRIBUTIONS

Significant contributions to music theory were made in the mid-20th century by several investigators who may be classified as symbolists, though most of them exhibited formalist, expressionist, and psychological elements as well. Some of the most influential (and controversial) work was done by Langer. Her most adamant critics (such as John Hospers) objected to her use of the term "symbol," which, in their lexica, must stand for something definite; she took pains to ascribe this more limited usage to the term "signal." The more general use of the term "symbol" that she endorsed already had a long history, notably in such 19th-century figures as Goethe, Thomas Carlyle, and the French Symbolist poets. Langer was accused of having somewhat weakened her argument through a vacillating terminology, and she described the musical symbol as "unconsummated" because of its ambiguity. But the validity of her theory did not depend upon the term "symbol"; her thought, indeed, had much in common with that of Edmund Gurney, who did not employ the term and whose ideal motion, if substituted for "symbol," would remove most of her critics' objections. Her use of "symbol" was nevertheless defensible; she construed art as a "symbolic analogue of emotive life," rendering the "forms of sentient being" into intelligible configurations. She was a naturalist; she saw art as organic in origin, and she echoed the view, long held among symbolists, that artistic form and content compose an indissoluble unity that each art manifests according to its peculiar conditions. The symbolism of music, she contended, is therefore tonal (or, at its broadest, auditory) in character and can be realized only in time; in psychological experience, time assumes an ideal guise. (Painting and sculpture, in their distinctive modalities, embody ideal space.) Langer embraced all the arts in her purview.

The American music theorist Gordon Epperson applied her concepts, with modifications, intensively to music in *The Musical Symbol* (1967).

CONTEXTUALIST THEORIES

In moving from symbolic to contextualist explanations of music, it is well to note that a source of great confusion, in the former, is the fact that tone painting (with explicit signals that yield, when the code is understood, designative meanings) is widely regarded as musical symbolism. An example of such tone painting is Bach's introduction of musical notes, corresponding to the letters of his own name, as a theme in the unfinished final fugue of the *Art of the Fugue*. And surely it may be argued that this qualifies on one level. But the contention that there is an intrinsic symbolism in the musical meaning itself is a claim that referentialists are generally unwilling to honour. Yet many theorists, whose concern is with the sociological or psychological effects of music, are not so much opposed to the idea of inner or profound meaning as indifferent to such meaning per se. Even an absolutist, however, is unable to examine music in isolation from its human environment. Meyer deliberately eschewed logical and philosophical problems of music and made "no attempt to decide whether music is a language or whether musical stimuli are signs or symbols." (He did not defend the inference that such concerns are irrelevant to meaning.) Musical meaning and communication, he maintained, cannot exist in the absence of the cultural context. The statement is hardly open to dispute; theorists are classified according to their proximity to the referential or nonreferential pole. If referentialists emphasize explicit aims and associations of a particular work (as in varieties of *Gebrauchsmusik,* or "utility" music, written for specific social or educational purposes), formalists can maintain that there is also an intrinsic, or embodied, meaning to which they attach the greater aesthetic value.

Among contextualists, however, a simple referential view is the exception rather than the rule. Any theorists who examine musical perception are studying a complex human activity. They are dealing with the psychology of music, in which certain elements—e.g., music, listener, mode of apprehension, cultural context—are indispensable and in which characteristic processes recur. Specialists will emphasize one element or another: formalists the music itself, sociologists the listeners and their milieu, psychologists the how of perception. Though psychology could survey the whole field, in practice psychologists, according to their persuasions, investigate the perception of measurable acoustic phenomena, the physical-mental effects of musical sound, or—more rarely—the functional role of music in human experience, and pragmatists and analysts alike may leave something out of account. But it remains for the comprehensive theorist, probably one who, like Langer, is equipped to discern relationships among many departments of thought, to construct a valid hierarchical structure of musical meaning in all its ramifications.

Deryck Cooke, the British musicologist and the author of *The Language of Music* (1959), who may be classified as a referential expressionist, offered a sophisticated argument for the notion of music as language. Concepts, however, may not be rendered by this language, only feelings. Cooke reaffirmed the possibility, long disputed by many theorists, that such feelings may be recognized, identified, and even classified. But he confined his investigation to the last few hundred years of the Western tradition.

INFORMATION THEORY

The French theorist Abraham Moles's *Information Theory and Esthetic Perception* (1966) brought the science of information theory to bear on musical perception, emphasizing that the concept of form is the essential thing; the "sonic message," whose dimensions vary from one composition to another, is a whole. Information theory thus proved to be a novel ally for organicists. The message, which is subjected to atomistic study of its components, is (thanks to recording) concrete; there is a temporal sonic material, a materia musica. Moles gave reinforcement to the aesthetic theory of distance:

> *The esthetic procedure of isolating sonic objects is analogous to the sculptor's or decorator's isolating a marble work against a black velvet draping: This procedure directs attention to it, alone and not as one element among many in a complex framework.*

Information theory, which Leonard Meyer also discussed, begins its investigations without the help of traditional theory, which it finds to be untenable for its procedures. Musical messages discerned through information theory are not referential, yet Moles chose to describe the measurable elements in the sonic repertoire as symbols: "each definable temporal stage represents a 'symbol' analogous to a phoneme in language." According to Moles, music must, as an art, obey rules; the role of aesthetics is to enumerate universally valid rules, not to perpetuate the arbitrary or merely traditional. He foresaw experimentation with a much richer repertoire of sounds, transcending musical instruments and drawing on whatever sources—certainly electronic ones—are available for realizing the "most general orchestra." A host of composers set out to fulfill this desideratum. In order to increase the compass of possible sounds, various electronic synthesizers were constructed. In electronically synthesized music, the medium itself is indistinguishable from its message.

The quest for some distillation of musical meaning may be foredoomed to failure. Meanings, intrinsic and extrinsic, abound; meanings of all kinds, moreover, are revealed in and through the social setting. Church, theatre, and broadcasting affect music in characteristic ways. The modern concert is a device whereby formal, autonomous meanings are emphasized; further, the scope and available repertoire of the concert have been enormously increased through recordings, for any suitably equipped room may become, at the turn of a switch, a recital hall.

CONSIDERATIONS RELATED TO PERFORMANCE PRACTICE

Listening to music for its own sake, apart from ritual or storytelling, is a relatively recent historical development. There have always been impromptu song and dance, and performances of music at home, in church, and in theatrical productions have a long history, but there was no public opera house

Venice's opera house, La Fenice Theatre, seen here in 2003, was a major Italian music centre for centuries. Although the structure was severely damaged by fire in 1996, it was reconstructed and reopened within a few years.

until 1637, when the first one opened in Venice. The first public concerts for which admission was charged appeared in London in 1672. During the next 50 years there were beginnings in Germany and France also, but the modern concert was not a significant feature of musical life until the late 18th century.

Of the forms that have characterized distinct periods of music history, it is sufficient to remark here that the chief Renaissance forms—mass, motet, the polyphonic chanson, and madrigal—were allied to texts that strongly influenced their structure. Instrumental music was for the most part in the service of the voice, though instrumental church compositions, dances, and chansons arranged for organ were not uncommon.

A strong alliance between voices and

CHANSON

French for "song," a chanson is a French art song of the Middle Ages and the Renaissance. The chanson before 1500 is preserved mostly in large manuscript collections called chansonniers.

Dating back to the 12th century, the monophonic chanson reached its greatest popularity with the trouvères of the 13th century, and can still be found in the mid-14th-century lais (a verse-song form) of the composer and poet Guillaume de Machaut. Only the melodies survive. The monophonic chansons show the development of intricate musico-poetic forms deriving from the songs of the slightly earlier counterparts of the trouvères, the troubadours. These forms were eventually simplified to become the *formes fixes* ("fixed forms") of the accompanied chanson.

The accompanied chanson—for a solo voice with written parts for one or more accompanying instruments—dominated French song from Machaut until Hayne van Ghizeghem and Antoine Busnois at the end of the 15th century. Almost all accompanied chansons adhere to one of the three *formes fixes*: ballade, rondeau, or virelai. The style is sophisticated, and the songs are evidently written for a court audience with high artistic aspirations and a cultivated taste. The general subject matter was courtly love.

The chanson for vocal ensemble had several antecedents. A chanson designed for two or three had appeared; around 1460 the polytextual chanson was in evidence, with two or more singers singing different texts simultaneously. By the end of the 15th century composers were beginning to look to a new kind of chanson texture. The work of the Flemish composer Josquin des Prez shows the gradual change to a style of chanson with four voices singing the same text, sometimes in melodic imitation but also in a homophonic (chordal) style.

In the next century the four-voice style gave way to five and six. Although the *formes fixes* of the previous two centuries were no longer used, the formal control and standard patterns of the chansons separates them from the Italian madrigals of the same years. Only later, in the work of Adriaan Willaert and Jacques Arcadelt (both of whom also wrote madrigals) did the styles begin to merge as the formal design of the chanson became less strictly reliant on balanced phrases and repeated material and more determined by the melodic imitation as a basis for structure.

(continued on the next page)

(continued from the previous page)

The later years of the 16th century saw the perfection of the polyphonic (multipart, usually with interwoven melodic lines) chanson in the work of Orlando di Lasso; and they saw the more homophonic style influenced by the attempt to match words to music in the measured verse *à l'antique* proposed by the members of La Pléiade (a French society seeking a return to Classical poetry and music) exemplified in the work of Claude Le Jeune. After 1600 the chanson yielded to a new kind of song: the *air de cour* for solo voice with lute accompaniment.

instruments has continued into the present, with musical theatre, the art song, and religious music. Instrumental music as a separate genre emerged in the 16th century, gaining considerable momentum in the 17th through a variety of idiomatic pieces. Increased attention to technical fluency was accompanied by greater complexity and sophistication in the instruments themselves. In response to stylistic demands for greater resonance and power, the modern forms of the violin appeared in the late 16th century, only gradually supplanting the earlier viols. The harpsichord did not finally yield to the pianoforte until the 18th century. The once-prevalent idea that early stringed and keyboard instruments were primitive precursors of their modern counterparts has been effectually demolished by research in medieval and Renaissance music and by dedicated performers, who seek to restore the sounds and spirit of those eras.

The development of opera, oratorio, and the cantata gave a prominence to vocal music throughout the Baroque era (c. 1600–1750) that made it equal in importance to instrumental music, with which these forms were closely allied. But instrumental chamber and independent orchestral ensembles, as they exist today, also had their beginnings during this period. A highly significant development of the late 18th century was the definitive appearance of the modern sonata (whether in the form of the solo and duo sonata, piano trio, string quartet, concerto, or symphony) with the Viennese classicists Haydn and Mozart and, later, Beethoven.

Since a vocal text is likely to be confused with intrinsic musical meaning, or at least to divert attention from a preoccupation with it, it is not surprising that aesthetic theory has followed on the emergence of an autonomous instrumental music requiring greater concentration on the sound itself, its colour and intensity, and the intelligibility (in terms of tonal organization alone) of a composition.

Moreover, the very concept of listening as an attentive (and sometimes rigorous), serious, and necessary activity of the music lover gained acceptance only slowly, following the inauguration of public concerts, and is still vigorously resisted. The expectation that the art should provide enjoyment without effort is, indeed, widespread and accounts for much of the opposition to new and demanding idioms. But even for well-disciplined and eager listeners there is the problem of quantity: they must cope as best they can with what Langer has called "the madhouse of too much art." If more effort is required, more discrimination is also needed. In music education, articulate voices ask that teaching be centred more upon qualitative aspects of the art ("aesthetic education"), less upon music making as an activity. This concern for musical value appears to reflect a more intensive search for meaning, which is not likely to be the exclusive property of a particular style or era, nor is it to be sought in an indiscriminate acceptance or rejection of novelty per se.

A pronounced pedagogical interest developed in various genres of popular music, such as rock, soul, and similar idioms with great numbers of followers, especially among the young, whose gigantic festivals generated feelings of religious exaltation. The lyrics of the songs are highly emotional and deal with a broad range of themes, from political protest to calls for a loud and lively dance party;

accompaniments are provided by guitars, keyboards, and percussion instruments and are electronically amplified. Music educators were attracted by the intrinsic structural values of this music, especially its distinctive rhythmic and modal characteristics, its texts, and the qualitative levels that may be distinguished. A music so vital and widespread, moreover, was deemed by many to be worth studying in school. In the mid-20th century the rock music movement emerged as a musical-sociological phenomenon of large proportions. Within a few decades, programs in popular music had been established in many postsecondary institutions, and by the early 21st century musicologists, music theorists, and educators in various disciplines were actively involved in the study of virtually every major genre of popular music across the globe.

MUSIC AND WORLDVIEW

Again, music proves its protean susceptibilities in the service of disparate worldviews. Among humanist psychologists (such as the Americans Gordon Allport and Abraham Maslow) music may be one among other means toward self-fulfillment, integration, self-actualization; for aesthetic existentialists (such as the philosopher Jean-Paul Sartre) it is yet another crucial department of choice and freedom; for spiritual existentialists (such as the philosophers Karl Jaspers and Martin Buber) it transmits transcendent overtones. For expressionists (such as the composers Schoenberg, Ernst Krenek, and René Leibowitz) music carries austere, and sometimes doctrinaire, moral imperatives. Theodor Adorno, a composer-philosopher and pupil of Alban Berg, wrote powerfully of these and spoke for an awareness of dazzling lucidity, but the tone, notwithstanding his humour, was one of obligation. Only the expressionists, among those mentioned here, were committed primarily to music, though Adorno, in particular, considered music and musicians always in interaction with their environments. The aesthetic concept of play is virtually absent, except among such humanists as Maslow. With Sartre, no less a humanist, the tone was one of responsibility. Many educators long held the explicit aim (at least in part because of a misinterpretation of John Dewey) of presenting the content of a discipline as "fun"; the concern for aesthetic education, an area of great interest to Dewey himself, eschewed this trivial view. But play, in the aesthetic sense, follows rules, as information theory has demonstrated; even controlled aleatory composition observes some limits. And the play may be very serious indeed, as in the important 20th-century atonal style known as 12-tone technique, practiced by the Viennese expressionists and their successors.

TONALITY AND MEANING

The most troublesome problem not only for the untutored listener but also for the professional musician has been, in much contemporary work, the loss of explicit tonality, and this accounts for the tardy popular response to Schoenberg and his school: the vocabulary is esoteric. Nineteenth-century compositions did, indeed, stretch the tonal system to its outer limits, but it is now clear that Wagner and Richard Strauss, and even the early Schoenberg, had not broken from it. As for Claude Debussy, his use of "exoticisms" was filigree upon a secure tonal base. So were such practices as the juxtaposition of keys by Stravinsky. This is not to say that the tonality of the Western world, fecund though it has been, is superior or more natural than other systems. Ethnomusicology has proved this to be a parochial view, though there are still those who champion harmonic practices based on the physical laws governing overtones—as Western tonality is—as the only "natural" source of development. It should not be irrelevant, however, to inquire if any folk music exhibits atonal characteristics.

Tonality in Western music, though a significant aspect, cannot be considered the crux of musical meaning. The tone rows that are used in the 12-tone compositions of Schoenberg, like major and minor tonality in

ETHNOMUSICOLOGY

Ethnomusicology is a field of scholarship that encompasses the study of all world musics from various perspectives. It is defined either as the comparative study of musical systems and cultures or as the anthropological study of music. Although the field had antecedents in the 18th and early 19th centuries, it began to gather energy with the development of recording techniques in the late 19th century. It was known as comparative musicology until about 1950, when the term ethnomusicology was introduced simultaneously by the Dutch scholar of Indonesian music Jaap Kunst and by several American scholars, including Richard Waterman and Alan Merriam. In the period after 1950, ethnomusicology burgeoned at academic institutions. Several societies and periodicals were founded, the most notable being the Society for Ethnomusicology, which publishes the journal *Ethnomusicology*.

Some ethnomusicologists consider their field to be associated with musicology, while others see the field as related more closely to anthropology. Among the general characteristics of the field are dependence on field research, which may include the direct study of music performance, and interest in all types of music produced in a society, including folk, art, and popular genres. Among the field's abiding concerns are whether outsiders can validly study another culture's music and what the researcher's obligations are to his informants, teachers, and consultants in colonial and postcolonial contexts. Over time, ethnomusicologists have gradually abandoned the detailed analytical study of music and increased their focus on the anthropological study of music as a domain of culture. With this shift in emphasis has come greater concern with the study of popular musics as expressions of the relationships between dominant and minority cultures; of music as a reflection of political, social-ethnic, and economic movements; and of music in the context of the cultural meanings of gender.

earlier music, are a technical substratum and must be no more explicit in the finished work than the chemical makeup of pigments in the *Mona Lisa.* The devices selected may affect the comprehensibility or accessibility of the work, but they are not, per se, the determinants of its worth or quality. Similarly with musical colour, or timbre; the 19th century produced a great profusion of compositions, particularly in the orchestral repertoire (e.g., works by Liszt and Berlioz) that exploited the unique sonorities of instruments; control of volume was, in itself, a rich source of colour. Works with literary or other extramusical associations were excellent vehicles for sonorous effects, but colour, like tonality, must be evaluated in musical context. Most notably, Langer, among other 20th-century aestheticians, regarded words themselves as musical, rather than discursive, ingredients; they are "assimilated" by the song.

CHAPTER THREE

MUSIC RECORDING

Because music evaporates as soon as it is produced, humans, seeking permanence in life's ephemera have long sought ways to create a physical record that can be reproduced and played back. The efforts to capture the fleeting sounds of music have followed two basic methods: that of symbols and that of signals. The former—musical notation—matured earlier, and in one form or another it virtually monopolized the recording of music for centuries; the latter had to await the emergence of technology for its development. In notation, symbols are written down as a message to a trained performing musician who understands them and reinterprets them into sound. Signals, on the other hand—being direct physical impressions of, and potential stimuli to, sounds—bypass the performer in their reproduction and, in some electronic compositions, even in their recording. This chapter concerns itself solely with the latter, nonsymbolic, method.

TYPES OF REPRODUCTION

The physical reproduction of music has been accomplished in three major ways, which can be designated the mechanical, the acoustical, and the electrical. In the mechanical, an automatic instrument, such as the barrel organ, plays music that has been built, or programmed, into the mechanism by the designer; the resulting sound is that of the apparatus. In the acoustical and electrical methods of reproduction, sonic vibrations themselves are captured in performance and reproduced—by purely mechanical means in the acoustical method and by the use of vacuum tubes, transistors, and other such devices in the electrical. In both cases, the resulting sound is expected to be that of the independent performance.

Until the end of the 19th century, music was reproduced primarily by means of the mechanical method. There are reports of other methods, probably based on the action of wind or forced air, dating as far back as about 1500 BCE, in the 18th dynasty of ancient Egypt, when a colossal statue of the god Memnon at Thebes made some sort of sounds to greet his mother, the goddess of the dawn. (Toppled by an earthquake in the year 27, the statue seems to have lost this ability upon reconstruction.) Friar Roger Bacon is reported to have invented some sort of talking head in the Middle Ages, and Josef Faber created in Vienna in 1860 a talking man with ivory reeds for vocal cords, a rubber tongue and lips, and with a keyboard that altered the mouth cavity to control word formation. The most common technique, however, called for a human hand or clockwork to turn a cylinder embedded with pins that would strike or otherwise operate some sound-producing apparatus, such as the metal teeth of a music-box comb; the hammers, quills, or pipes of a keyboard instrument; or the clappers of a set of bells. Automatic carillons are known from the 1300s; automatic harpsichords and organs, from the 1500s. King Henry VIII of England owned an automatic virginal; his daughter Queen Elizabeth I in 1593 sent the sultan of Turkey an elaborate musical clock. Every six hours it played a tune on 16 chimes, followed by a two-trumpet tantara, then by an organ tune and performance by "a holly bushe full of birds and thrushes, which at the end of the musick did singe and shake theire winges." In the 19th century Queen Victoria of Great Britain owned a bustle that would play "God Save the Queen" when she sat down.

GLAVICIMBAL.

Wann Orgel und Regal zu starck bey Music Chören
  so diene ich vergnügt; des Clavicimbels Schall
läßt durch die Wunder Faust auch Wunder dinge hören
  es dringt durch Hertz und Ohr den angenehme Hall.
kommt eine schöne Fug und rare Phantasien
  so muß was sonst betrübt in Augenblick entfliehen.

Man playing harpsichord, 18th–century engraving by German artist Christoph Weigel the Elder

Some of the most illustrious composers in the history of music wrote for mechanical devices. Haydn wrote tunes for musical (pipe organ) clocks; Mozart wrote several pieces for mechanical organ; and Beethoven wrote his Wellington's Victory (or Battle Symphony) for the panharmonicon, a full mechanical orchestra invented by Johann Nepomuk Maelzel (Mälzel), a German musician who perfected the metronome.

At the end of the 19th century, two inventions superseded the barrel-and-pin mechanism. One was the player piano, which used a perforated cardboard roll to control a stream of air that activated the piano's hammers. This had the advantage of enabling pianists to record their performances for future playback, and many virtuosos and composers took advantage of this device, among them Ignacy Paderewski, Edvard Grieg, Claude Debussy, and Sergey Rachmaninoff. Some composers, including Igor Stravinsky and Paul Hindemith, wrote music especially for the piano roll, using devices such as combinations of as many as 30 notes played simultaneously; while impossible for two hands, such chords could readily be played by the perforated paper.

The second invention, which was to make obsolete all previous music-reproducing apparatuses (except in toys and cuckoo clocks), was the phonograph.

THE PHONOGRAPH

Also called a record player, the phonograph is an instrument for reproducing sounds by means of the vibration of a stylus, or needle, following a groove on a rotating disc. A phonograph disc, or record, stores a replica of sound waves as a series of undulations in a sinuous groove inscribed on its rotating surface by the stylus. When the record is played back, another stylus responds to the undulations, and its motions are then reconverted into sound.

Though experimental mechanisms of this type appeared as early as 1857, the invention of the phonograph is generally credited to the American inventor Thomas Edison (1877). His first recordings were indentations embossed into a sheet of tinfoil by a vibrating stylus; the tinfoil was wrapped around a cylinder that was rotated as the sounds were being recorded. Improvements in Edison's process followed, notable among which were Emil Berliner's innovation in 1887 of tracing sound grooves in a spiral on a flat disc rather than in a helix on a cylinder. A negative was made from the flat master disc, and the negative then used as a mold for making many copies that reproduced the original master disc. These "records," as they came to be known, could be played on a reproducing machine Berliner named a Gramophone. Improved methods of molding disc records followed in the early 20th century, and by 1915 the 78-RPM (revolutions-per-minute) record, with a playing time of about 4 and a half minutes per side, had become standard. In the early 1920s electric loudspeakers were adopted to amplify the volume of reproduced sound. In 1948 Columbia Records introduced the long-playing (LP) record, which, with a rotational speed of 33 $1/3$ RPM and the use of very fine grooves, could yield up to 30 minutes of playing time per side. Shortly afterward RCA Corporation introduced the 45-RPM disc, which could play for up to 8 minutes per side. These LPs and "singles" supplanted 78s in the 1950s, and stereophonic (or "stereo") systems, with two separate channels of information in a single groove, became a commercial reality in 1958. Stereo phonographs capable of the undistorted reproduction of sound became one component of what is known as a high-fidelity sound system.

Teens in the 1960's listen to music on a record player.

(continued on the next page)

(continued from the previous page)

All modern phonograph systems had certain components in common: a turntable that rotated the record; a stylus that tracked a groove in the record; a pickup that converted the mechanical movements of the stylus into electrical impulses; an amplifier that intensified these electrical impulses; and a loudspeaker that converted the amplified signals back into sound.

Phonographs and records were the chief means of reproducing recorded sound at home until the 1980s, when they were largely supplanted by recorded cassettes and compact discs (which, in turn, were replaced by computers, MP3 players, smartphones, and the like).

THE INFLUENCE OF RECORDING

In 1967 a survey of hundreds of American composers indicated that they were almost unanimous in regarding the recordings of their works as being more important than either printed publication or live performances. Through recordings, composers gained not only an easy familiarity with the music of others but also a new medium for their own works.

COMPOSITION

The contemporary American composer and teacher Milton Babbitt, in a conversation in 1965 with the Canadian pianist Glenn Gould (who maintained his own reputation largely by means of records and broadcasts, rather than by concert performances), said:

> *We have all been affected as composers, as teachers, as musicians by recordings to an extent that cannot possibly be calculated as yet . . . I don't think one can possibly exaggerate the extent to which the climate of music today is determined by the fact that the total Webern is available on records, that the total Schoenberg is becoming available.*

The use of the record as a medium had superficial beginnings as early as 1904 in Ruggero Leoncavallo's song "Mattinata," specifically written for the record according to the label. Later, in 1925, Stravinsky composed a piano piece, *Serenade in A Major*, expressly for the record medium, though it is also perfectly capable of being performed live. Ottorino Respighi's *Pines of Rome* (1924) incorporates a recording of a nightingale's song in its third movement. Much more important use of recording as a medium occurred toward mid-century in works fundamentally relying on recorded tape, such as Edgard Varèse's *Poème électronique*, an 11-channel tape played through 425 speakers at the 1958 Brussels World Fair, and Morton Subotnick's *Silver Apples of the Moon* (1967), an electronic work playable only as a recording.

TEACHING

In music education the phonograph was early adopted as a tool in teaching both serious students and laymen. Teachers who could not adequately illustrate musical examples at the piano found in records a means of demonstration. They could also bring entire orchestras into the classroom by means of the phonograph.

In 1930 the *Columbia History of Music by Ear and Eye*, a phonographic survey that became popular in music history classes, enabled many students—as well as many of their teachers—to hear for the first time such instruments as viols, lutes, virginals, clavichords, and harpsichords together with the then little-known music written for them. A half-dozen years later another educational recorded project, *L'Anthologie sonore*, added impetus to this specialized field. By the 1960s the Baroque music of the 17th and 18th centuries—as well as the earlier music of the Renaissance and medieval era—increasingly was recorded in performances using the instruments for which it was written. Such music found a wide audience beyond educational institutions; this audience was developed in large part by the phonograph.

By the late 20th century many conservatories, colleges, and universities, and even some secondary schools, had constructed recording studios to enable students to analyze their own performances or to rehear their own compositions.

CRITICISM

Records also enabled music critics to expand their knowledge and perspective of music and performance practices. Unfortunately, a record collection also allows reviewers to write on superficial differences between performances with very little expenditure of intellectual energy. New music has suffered especially from the resulting loss of the ability of many critics to expostulate on music for their readers.

CONCERTS

The impact of recordings on the concert hall has also been enormous, both for classical and for popular performances. Performers today can hardly hope to attract a concert audience if they have not produced distinguished recordings; usually, their audiences, both at home and abroad, consist of persons who know the performers' work through recordings. In the popular music field especially, many performers cannot compete in live appearances with recordings in which they depend heavily on technical aid. When the phonograph first appeared on the scene, there were some who felt that it might cause the demise of live performance in the concert hall, or, if it survived at all, assuming it would do so for social rather than musical reasons.

Years later, after the various incarnations of recorded music—whether bought, streamed, or

legitimately downloaded—are at record (no pun intended) lows, the concert has become all-important again for performers, as it is the only sure source of income.

The American Symphony Orchestra, conducted by music director Leon Botstein, plays "Richard Strauss Choral Works" at Avery Fisher Hall in New York City in 2005.

MUSICOLOGY

The entire field of comparative musicology—i.e., the study of the relationships between Western, non-Western, and primitive music—depends upon disc and tape recordings. Although the discipline may be traced to the 18th century, it did not emerge from a primitive state until it acquired phonographic tools. Primitive music is generally transmitted orally rather than through a written tradition, and as such its performance practices—certainly in rhythm and intonation—cannot be accurately transcribed into Western notation. Since World War II anthropologists and musicologists have visited the most remote parts of the world with recording devices to record aboriginal music before it was either tainted or wiped out by Western civilization. While studies in the sixties were conducted in a "race against time," fearing the homogenizing effects of the then-ubiquitous transistor radio, today's multitude of online sources offer up a vast array of music that is anything but homogenous.

THE ROLE OF THE PRODUCER

Although the record producer has at times become an equal partner with the musicians in creating the recorded performance of

classical music, in the popular field he or she
is frequently in total command. Here, in fact,
the sounds produced by the musicians may
simply be the raw material with which the
producer works; artificial sounds, overlays of
sound upon sound, electronically introduced
reverberation, multichannel effects with direc-
tional interplay and moving instruments, all
may serve as vital ingredients of the recording.
Paradoxically, as technological advancement
brought the recording beyond the mere imitation of live performances, popular musicians
began to bring complex electronic equipment
into the concert halls to imitate the sounds of
their recordings.

In productions of classical music, serious
thought is given to whether the recording
should faithfully capture the performance
as heard from the optimum position in
the concert hall or studio or whether the
recording setup should be used to "enhance"
the performance. Few question any longer
the common practice of correcting actual
mistakes. Ever since magnetic tape made
detailed editing possible, extra takes have
been made of sections in which musical
problems are evident. The best taping of
each section is spliced into a master tape.
Even in recordings made during an actual
concert, performers sometimes return to the
hall afterward to emend any blemishes. The
improvements in recorded performances

made possible by tape splicing, however, often misled audiences into anticipating the same perfection in live performances. Also, although tape editing facilitated the excision of poor passages that, while acceptable in the heat of a concert, would become irritating upon repeated hearings, it was also said to have hampered the continuity of the performance. It is unlikely, however, that listeners then were able to spot the rare movement that required no splicing from the majority that did. This alleged lack of continuity, however, was much worse when music had to be recorded in five-minute segments, for recordings at 78 revolutions per minute (rpm). (Detailed coverage of how recorded music began and then advanced to what it is today is covered in the next section of this chapter, The Development of Musical Recording.)

Microphone placement has been perhaps the major criterion in separating the "natural" or "re-creative" from the "creative" technique of large-scale classical recordings. In a natural setup microphones are placed in the optimum positions in the hall—often directly over the conductor—in order to re-create the concert-hall or opera-house effect. In the natural arrangement the conductor is responsible for instrumental and vocal balances.

Some record-producing companies prefer to put microphones closer to the performers—this is called close-miking technique. Here the record producer—generally with the final approval of the conductor or leader—is responsible for balances, for bringing out particular instrumental or vocal lines; in other words, the producer participates in the interpretation. Studio-made popular recordings—other than those of a lush semiclassical nature—have generally used the close-miking technique; in some cases, each performer in a small musical group is assigned his own microphone. In a close-miked symphonic recording session, as many as 18 microphones may be used: three for violins; one for cellos and basses (sometimes one for each); one each for woodwinds, brasses, timpani, snare drum and triangle, bass drum and cymbals, celesta or harp, and soloist; and from three to six for a chorus. Several separate recordings, or "tracks," each comprising the inputs of several microphones, generally are made at the same time, and the producer must balance the strength of these various inputs during the recording session. Until about 1960 two-track machines were ordinarily used; by 1970 eight-track recorders were in use, allowing much more subtle mixing of channels during the editing sessions subsequent to the actual recording. For popular music sessions 16-track recorders are sometimes used. For stereophony all the recording tracks must be edited and mixed to make the final two channels. The record producer also determines the degree of separation between those two channels, and during a dramatic recording—an opera, for example—he may function as stage director in guiding the performers around the aural stage.

In quadraphony (quadriphony), which has four channels and which, in disc format, unsuccessfully tried to find a market in the early 1970s, the controversy between natural and close-miked recordings persisted. In classical music, when the two rear channels were used mainly for hall ambience, the arguments centred on the placement of the two front channels. Some companies, however, began to use the four channels as equal partners even in the classics. Columbia, for example, sometimes placed the conductor in the middle of the orchestra, which was seated for optimum quadraphonic array rather than for optimum concert-hall effect. In the early 1970s several quadraphonic disc systems competed for prominence, most notably Columbia's SQ, Japan Victor Company's CD-4 (RCA's Quadradisc in the United States), and Sansui's RM (also called QS). Since they were incompatible systems, confused consumers, waiting for one to become standard, withheld their votes from all, and by the end of the decade the aural and aesthetic benefits of quadraphony had all but disappeared from the marketplace.

THE DEVELOPMENT OF MUSICAL RECORDING

In 1877 the U.S. inventor Thomas Alva Edison heard "Mary had a little lamb" emanate from a machine into which he had just spoken the ditty. It was the first time a recording of the human voice had been reproduced, and the event signaled the birth of the phonograph.

Edison sent representatives, machines, and cylinders to Europe almost as soon as he had invented the phonograph, and between 1888 and 1894 recordings were made by such notables as Alfred, Lord Tennyson, Robert Browning, and even Johannes Brahms, who played a Hungarian rhapsody. The first "celebrity" recording, however, was made in Edison's West Orange, New Jersey, laboratories when the pianist Josef Hofmann, then a 12-year-old prodigy, paid a visit to Edison's studio in 1888. Hans von Bülow followed shortly after with a recording of a Chopin mazurka on the piano.

In 1894 Charles and Émile Pathé built a small phonograph factory in a suburb of Paris and began to record singers as eminent as Mary Garden. Within a decade their catalog boasted some 12,000 items, and their name became almost synonymous with the cylinder phonograph in Europe. Meanwhile, Emile Berliner, a German immigrant living in Washington, D.C., had filed a patent in 1887 for a

"Gramophone," using a disc rather than a cylinder, and he began manufacturing Gramophones and discs in 1894. The disc had the commercial advantage of being more easily manufactured than the cylinders. One of his representatives established a branch in London, the Gramophone Company (in 1898), a branch in Berlin, Deutsche Grammophon AG, and one in France, the Compagnie Français du Gramophone, while Berliner's brother set up a disc-pressing facility in Hannover. Most of Europe's recording industry thus was started by Berliner's representatives, and in the United States the small Berliner organization was to turn into the giant Victor company.

By the beginning of the 20th century, recording industries had been established in Germany, Austria, Russia, and Spain. Much of the managerial and technical talent, not to mention equipment, had been imported from America. (By 1970, the positions would be reversed, with Europe in command of most of the American market.) Today, although independent labels certainly have their share of the market, corporations have a huge and controlling stake in the industry. The big three are Sony Music Entertainment (Japan), Universal Music Group (France), and Warner Music Group (the United States).

It may be hard to imagine that in the 1890s, recordings had become popular primarily through coin-in-the-slot phonographs, which were stationed in various in public places. Talent was incidental to the novelty of the apparatus; most of the recordings were of whistlers, bands, comic numbers, ditties, ethnic routines, and the like. In the first years of the 20th century, Victor and its affiliates raised cultural expectations with its Red Seal series (Red Label in Europe), particularly with discs made, beginning in 1902, by Enrico Caruso. By 1910 the vast majority of record sales—some estimates are as high as 85 percent—were classical.

The Red Label had been initiated in 1901 in Russia with some of the first 10-inch disc recordings made, and the basso Fyodor Chaliapin was among the first artists to record on the new Russian Red Label.

In 1902 Victor and another major label, Columbia, decided to help the development of the new industry by pooling their patents. Victor was thereby legally able to record on wax (which would then be electroplated) for the first time, and the new wax discs were then used in recording Caruso in Milan. Caruso's discs were a major catalyst in transforming the amusing gadget of a phonograph into a respected cultural phenomenon. That same year the new series received London-made recordings by stars of the Covent Garden opera house, primarily through the efforts of the Gramophone Company's music director, Landon Ronald, a bona fide serious musician

ENRICO CARUSO

Enrico Caruso, whose original name was Errico Caruso, (born February 25, 1873, Naples, Italy—died August 2, 1921, Naples), was the most admired Italian operatic tenor of the early 20th century and one of the first musicians to document his voice on gramophone recordings.

Caruso was born into a poor family. Although he was a musical child who sang Neapolitan folk songs everywhere and joined his parish choir at the age of nine, he received no formal music training until his study with Guglielmo Vergine at age 18. Within three years, in 1894, he made his operatic debut, in Mario Morelli's *L'Amico Francesco* in Naples at the Teatro Nuovo. Four years later, after adding a number of impressive roles to his repertoire, he was asked to create the role of Loris in the premiere of Umberto Giordano's *Fedora* in Milan. He was a sensation and soon had engagements in Moscow, St. Petersburg (Russia), and Buenos Aires. He made his La Scala debut with *La Bohème* (1900). In 1901, after being unfavourably received in his performance in *L'elisir d'amore* in Naples, he vowed never again to sing in Naples, and he kept his word.

(continued on page 90)

Caruso in 1903, as the duke of Mantua in
Giuseppe Verdi's *Rigoletto*

(continued from page 88)

Caruso then created the chief tenor parts in *Adriana Lecouvreur, Germania*, and *La fanciulla del West*, and for the La Scala company the tenor roles in *Le Maschere* and *L'elisir d'amore*. World recognition came in the spring of 1902 after he sang in *La Bohème* at Monte Carlo and in *Rigoletto* at London's Covent Garden. He made his American debut in *Rigoletto* at the opening night of the Metropolitan Opera in New York City on November 23, 1903, and continued to open each season there for the next 17 years, presenting 36 roles in all. His last public appearance—his 607th performance with the Metropolitan—was as Eléazar in *La Juive* (December 24, 1920).

Caruso became the most celebrated and highest paid of his contemporaries worldwide. He made recordings of about 200 operatic excerpts and songs; many of them are still being published. His voice was sensuous, lyrical, and vigorous in dramatic outbursts and became progressively darker in timbre in his later years. Its appealing tenor qualities were unusually rich in lower registers and abounded in warmth, vitality, and smoothness.

the English Columbia Graphophone Company divested itself of its near-defunct American progenitor and joined the Gramophone Company to form Electric and Musical Industries, Ltd. (EMI), bringing into the merger nearly every important European firm except DGG and its export label, Polydor. American Columbia was revived by its purchase, in 1938, by the Columbia Broadcasting System.

During the 1930s, as the American companies relied mainly on dance records in jukeboxes to satisfy a dwindled market, Europe supplied a slow but steady trickle of classical recordings. In 1931 the His Master's Voice (HMV) label in Great Britain began its "Society" issues: a limited public was asked to subscribe in advance to then esoteric releases—the complete Beethoven piano sonatas played by Artur Schnabel or Pablo Casals performing the Bach unaccompanied cello suites. A new British company, Decca, organized in 1929, also began to issue serious recordings. In the United States, Columbia began to record a number of distinguished orchestras, including those of New York City, Chicago, Cleveland, and Minneapolis. RCA retained its leadership, however, with the Philadelphia Orchestra under Eugene Ormandy, the Boston Symphony Orchestra under Serge Koussevitzky, and—perhaps the greatest orchestral combination ever assembled—the NBCE Symphony under Arturo Toscanini, as well as with the violinist Jascha Heifetz and the pianist Vladimir Horowitz.

ADVANCEMENTS FROM WORLD WAR II THROUGH THE 1980S

British Decca had a far-reaching role to play after World War II when its ffrr—full frequency range recording—became internationally known. The frequency range of discs had been dramatically extended, and Ernest Ansermet's recording of Stravinsky's *Petrushka* in the new process was to awaken the unsuspecting ears of many record collectors in 1946 to the future high fidelity, or "hi-fi," possibilities of the phonograph.

Two other developments in the late 1940s combined with the extended frequency range to produce a radical change in the development of recordings: magnetic recording and the first commercially successful long-playing (LP) record. In 1948 Columbia Records demonstrated 12-inch unbreakable vinyl discs that could play about 25 minutes of music per side. The standard shellac disc had revolved at 78 rpm, and a 12-inch disc had to be changed, automatically or manually, every five minutes, thus breaking up the continuity of longer works; the 12-inch LP, revolving at 33 1/3 rpm, could hold the average symphony, sonata, or quartet on a single side. And the vinyl discs had quieter surfaces than the shellac. Victor soon countered with its own microgroove records: seven-inch vinyl discs at 45 rpm. Each contained approximately as much music as a 12-inch 78-rpm disc, but the package was smaller. By 1950, a pattern had been set: 12-inch LPs for classical works and popular albums, 45s for individual popular songs. Extended-play 45s also were developed and successfully marketed. The LP opened up an entirely new market—not only newcomers but older record collectors who could see the advantage of the new technology and were willing to repurchase their collections as LPs. The 78-rpm shellac disc followed the cylinder into oblivion.

Tape had a major impact on recording starting in the late 1940s: anyone with a good recorder and microphone could become a record producer. Small companies sprang up in areas of music ignored by the giants: the esoteric and the avant-garde, the music of the periods before and after the highly popular Romantic classics of the 19th century. Chamber music, as well as Baroque works of the 18th century and earlier, which required paying fewer musicians than an entire symphony orchestra, flooded record stores and resulted in an unprecedented Baroque revival among music lovers. All-Vivaldi concerts were sold out, and Bach became a best-seller. Orchestral recordings of less familiar works—produced in a Europe that had been ravaged by World War II, where musicians' fees were minimal—crested the flood. New companies recorded for the first time many symphonies, quartets, masses, little-known operas, and many other once esoteric works, some of which were now available in competing versions. The more popular standard works, the symphonies of Beethoven, Brahms, and Tchaikovsky, became duplicated by the dozens. By the mid-1950s it seemed that most of the worthwhile musical output of Western civilization—and much from Asia and Africa—had been made available to the average home.

For a few owners of some deluxe tape recorders, a new listening experience was available by 1956: stereophonic tape recordings. Within two years stereo discs made their commercial appearance; every major U.S. company began issuing stereo discs by the end of 1958.

Now a new flood of records hit the market: notably popular were those that displayed the spectacular effects possible with stereo. It was again Decca/London that convinced the serious music lover of the musical benefits of stereo with the release in 1959 of Wagner's *Das Rheingold*, conducted by Georg (later Sir Georg) Solti, a pioneer work in the "creative" school of classical record production. Within a decade two complete recordings of Wagner's Ring cycle, comprising four complete operas on 19 discs, were available. Again, as with the advent of the LP, a technical advance spurred the record industry into recording an even greater repertoire than was available previously. By the late 1960s most American record companies had discontinued their monaural recordings, except for "historical reissues."

The 1950s saw a rearrangement of record company alliances, as Europe began its strong invasion of America. By the 1970s not only did Europe own a sizable chunk of the American record industry, but it had taken over the recording, for the first time, of many of the most prestigious U.S. orchestras.

Another far-reaching phenomenon of the 1950s was Elvis Presley, a popular U.S. singer who inspired a new, militantly youth-oriented style of music: rock and roll. It generated a multitude of solo singers and groups as well as a teenage and subteen culture of rabid record buyers. The success of the British rock group the Beatles helped stimulate record sales in the 1960s to an all-time high. The sales of classical records, however, represented a declining portion of the total. It seemed that most people who wanted the standard classics had already bought them and that few new standard works of any length were being written. Rather than new classical recordings, re-releases were issued in new packages (e.g., "Debussy's Greatest Hits") and in the new medium of tape. During the mid-1960s two small and conveniently packaged tape formats began a steady rise to popularity:

ELVIS PRESLEY

Few entertainers have rivaled the impact and the influence of Elvis Presley. Known as the "King of Rock and Roll," he was a central figure in merging country music and rhythm and blues to create rock in the mid-1950s. He remained a hugely popular performer into the 1970s, producing 45 records that sold more than a million copies each, appearing in 33 motion pictures, and performing in concerts throughout the United States. His death in 1977 in no way diminished his popularity. His records continued to sell, and his legend inspired a host of imitators.

Elvis Aaron (or Aron) Presley was born on January 8, 1935, in Tupelo, Mississippi. In 1949 the family moved to Memphis, Tennessee, where young Presley attended L.C. Humes High School, graduating in 1953. That summer he came to the attention of Sam Phillips, president of Sun Records, when he went there to make a personal recording as a present for his mother. Presley made his first commercial recording for Sun the following year.

The five Presley singles released by Sun in 1954-55, including "That's All Right Mama" and "Mystery Train," are among the most notable pop records of the 20th century. Their blend of country, rhythm and blues, and gospel became known as rockabilly, an early form of rock and roll. Although none of the Sun singles became a national hit, Presley attracted a substantial southern following with his recordings, his live appearances, and his radio performances.

In 1955 Presley came under the management of Colonel Tom Parker, who had made stars of the country music artists Eddy Arnold and Hank Snow. Parker arranged for Presley's recording contract to be sold from Sun to RCA Victor. Presley's recordings for RCA—including "Heartbreak Hotel," "Don't Be Cruel," "Love Me Tender" (all 1956), and "All Shook Up" (1957)—made him a national sensation. From 1956 through 1958 he dominated the best-seller charts and ushered in the age of rock and roll, opening doors for both white and black rock artists. His television appearances, especially those on Ed Sullivan's Sunday night variety show, set records for the size of the audiences. His hip gyrations, which some viewers thought too suggestive, earned him the nickname "Elvis the Pelvis."

Drafted into the U.S. Army in 1958, Presley went through regular training and then served as a truck driver in West Germany

(continued on page 103)

Elvis Presley up on his toes, performs onstage in 1956 at the Olympia Theater in downtown Miami, Fla.

(continued from page 101)

until his discharge in 1960. Resuming his career under Parker's supervision, he spent most of the 1960s filming lighthearted movies and recording their soundtracks. Presley did his best work of the decade on singles, such as "It's Now or Never ('O Sole Mio')" (1960), "Are You Lonesome Tonight?" (1961), "Can't Help Falling in Love" (1962), and "Viva Las Vegas" (1964). Faced with declining movie grosses and record sales, Presley performed in a one-man television special in 1968 that restored much of his artistic credibility. His comeback continued with the release of the single "Suspicious Minds" (1969), which went to number one.

Presley began touring again and won back a large audience. For much of the next decade he was again one of the top live attractions in the United States. No longer a controversial figure, Presley was now a mainstream American entertainer. He had married in 1967 and had become a parent with the birth of his daughter, Lisa Marie, in 1968; he was divorced in 1973. When not on the road Presley spent almost all of his time at Graceland, his lavish Memphis mansion, using it as a retreat from the enthusiasm of his fans. In his last years he gained weight and took a variety of prescription drugs. On August 16, 1977, he died of a heart attack brought on largely by drug abuse.

the continuous-loop one-reel cartridge and the two-reel cassette. Each obviated the need for threading tape in order to play it. The cartridge first achieved consumer acceptance as an automobile accessory and was designed primarily as a playback-only format; the cassette configuration was first introduced in an inexpensive portable recorder player.

Cassettes had the advantage over continuous-loop cartridges in being rewindable and thus easier to control for selective "spotting" and for amateur recording. For non-selective music or music in which it is not necessary to start at the beginning— background music, for instance—the continuous-loop cartridge had the advantage of not having to be rewound at all. In 1979 Sony introduced the Walkman, a personal stereo cassette player that made it possible for people to carry their music with them easily. By the end of 1982 sales of recorded music on cassettes had overtaken those of LP discs in the United States.

CAN YOU HEAR ME NOW?

Meanwhile, a new recording technique that boasted, among other things, a wider dynamic range had begun to revolutionize the market for quality recordings: The recording devices discussed thus far use analog technology— that is, they produce and store a physical representation (an "analog") of sound waves. Most modern recording, however, is done digitally. Digital recording analyzes an analog signal and samples, or measures, it thousands of times a second. Each of these samples is assigned a value, and that value is converted into binary number data (numbers containing only 0s and 1s). Binary numbers are easily stored, retrieved, and edited on computers and playback devices. Digital audio recordings

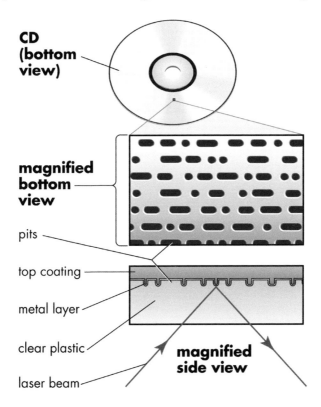

CD (bottom view)

magnified bottom view

pits

top coating

metal layer

clear plastic

laser beam

magnified side view

A laser beam reads information stored on a CD in a pattern made by tiny pits.

are free of the noise and distortion typical of analog recordings, thus offering a superior experience for the listener.

The first popular digital audio format was the compact disc (CD), which eclipsed the LP in popularity in the late 1980s. In addition to offering improved sound, CDs could store up to 80 minutes of recorded music on a side, while LPs offered only 60 or 70 minutes on two sides. In the late 1980s digital audio tape (DAT) recorders became available for sound recording and reproduction. Although DAT was meant to replace the cassette, the format never won wide acceptance.

The next milestone in digital audio was the introduction of digital audio files. The most popular type is the MP3, but various formats exist. Digital audio

Apple's fifth-generation iPod portable media player, 2005

files provide near-CD quality sound at vastly reduced file sizes. The size of CD audio files is reduced by discarding certain sounds based on assumptions of what the ear is least likely to miss. The smaller size made it feasible to download music files from the Internet and then listen to them on a computer or transfer them to a portable digital music player, such as Apple Inc.'s iPod. During the first decade of the 21st century digital downloads surpassed CDs in terms of units sold.

CHAPTER FOUR

MUSICAL GENRES OF NOTE

What did Neanderthals listen to? As there are no sonic equivalents to cave paintings, we have no way of knowing if music was a part of life some 100,000 to 300,000 years ago. We do, however, have information about various musical forms going back some 1500 years or so, beginning with classical music. As we move forward in time, various genres, some overlapping, will take center stage.

CLASSICAL MUSIC

The term "classical music" has several meanings. Music from the classical age—the Western historical period of Haydn, Mozart, and Beethoven—is classical music. In China classical music refers to the ancient Chinese music before the influence of Western art forms. In the West it has come to be a synonym for art music in contrast to popular and folk musics and is used here in this sense.

The Bible contains the words of many Hebrew songs and mentions such musical instruments as the harp, lyre, trumpet, and cymbal. Hebrew chants sung in the temple foreshadowed early Christian songs.

Among the Greeks the theory of music was highly developed. In the 6th century BCE the mathematician Pythagoras accurately determined the numerical relationships

More than 500 years old, Jewish music, written in Hebrew, gives testament to the ancient roots of musical performances. This particular document was made by putting pen, ink, tempera, and gold leaf to vellum.

between strings that produced tones of different pitches. The Greeks selected and arranged the tones in scales called modes. Two of these Greek modes supplied the foundation for the music of the Western world. Choruses played an integral part in the ancient Greek dramas, sometimes singing as well as speaking. Poet-musicians competed at religious festivals. The amateur players accompanied their poems on the lyre, and virtuosos used the cithara, a similar instrument with more strings.

THE MIDDLE AGES

The development of Western music was intertwined with the growth of the Christian church. Chanting of scriptures and prayers was practiced by early Christians. By the 6th century CE modal chant—known as plainchant—had increased so greatly that Pope Gregory I had it collected and organized, and it came to be called Gregorian chant. The chant did not have a regular rhythm but was fitted to the natural accents of the Latin words. Like all previous music, each chant consisted of a single melody, and all the singers sang the same notes. This type of music is called monophonic, or one-voiced.

Nonreligious, or secular, music was composed by wandering poets who sang of chivalry and courtly love in the 12th and

13th centuries. In France they were either jongleurs, itinerant minstrels who made a living from their songs, or troubadours and trouvères, aristocrats who sang for the love of music. In Germany the poet-musicians were called minnesingers. Some 2,000 minstrel melodies are preserved in old manuscripts.

The discovery that two voices could sing two separate melodies at the same time— and still produce pleasing sounds—occurred sometime during the 9th century. During the next four centuries this type of music gradually replaced the older monophonic style.

The first experiments in the new music were called organum. A second voice or voices sang the chant melody at perhaps an interval of a fourth or fifth above the original, or tenor. Sometimes the two moved in opposite directions. Above the tenor a more elaborate part might be sung. As the two parts became more independent, often two distinct melodies proceeded at the same time. When third and fourth parts were added, the music became truly polyphonic.

Sometime after the mid–12th century, a new Notre Dame Cathedral was being built in Paris, and with it grew a school of composers. Two names have been preserved from that school—Léonin and Pérotin. They stretched the organum to unheard-of lengths and embellished it with flourishes of long melismas, or many notes sung to one syllable. New rhythmic patterns developed, as did repetitions of motifs, sequential patterns, and imitation.

Out of this developed the motet, originally in Latin on a sacred text. Unlike the organum, the text was sung in the upper voices as well as the tenor. Bilingual motets (French-Latin, English-Latin) arose, and secular texts or combinations of sacred and secular texts were used. Tenors were sometimes chosen from French popular songs instead of from plainchant. Instruments played lower voice parts, making the motet an accompanied solo song.

The period culminated in the works of Guillaume de Machaut. He left 23 motets, more than 100 secular songs, and a mass. They are characterized by excellent craftsmanship with colourful melodic and harmonic inflections and constantly shifting rhythms.

THE RENAISSANCE

The period from the mid–15th century to about 1600 is usually subdivided into three ages: early, from about 1425 to 1490, the age of Guillaume Dufay and Jean d'Ockeghem; high (1490–1520), the age of Josquin des Prez; and late, the age of Giovanni Pierluigi da Palestrina. The period before 1550 has also been called the age of the Netherlanders, from the leading role played by composers of present-day Belgium, The Netherlands, and northern France. In the last half of the 16th century the mainstream of European polyphony was also represented by nationals other than the Italian Palestrina—especially William Byrd in England, Tomás Luis de Victoria in Spain, the Netherlander Orlando di Lasso in Germany, and Philippe de Monte in Austria.

The period from the mid-15th to the 17th century marked an amalgamation of the Netherlanders' and Italians' techniques, culminating in the music of Josquin. His influence was felt for the remainder of the era. In his works the elaborate polyphony of the north and the chordal, harmonically controlled style of the south are fused into a rich and expressive language—the perfect union of words and music.

The Italian madrigal was a relative latecomer in the Renaissance, the term in a title first appearing in 1530. It was intended as a return to an elevated style from antiquity but drew on the contemporary style of the sacred motet and on Josquin's sonorous chansons. The Netherlanders predominated at first, and it was not until the middle of the century that Italian composers began to contribute with a new and detailed expressiveness. It influenced all national secular part songs but found a special naturalized home in Elizabethan England with such composers as Byrd, Thomas Morley, John Wilbye, Thomas Weelkes, Orlando Gibbons, and Thomas Tomkins.

During the Renaissance, instrumental music freed itself from its dependence on vocal models and emerged as an individual style. Although it continued to be composed "apt for voices or viols," as the Elizabethans put it, music developed that reflected the capabilities of performers and the technical possibilities of instruments.

THE BAROQUE ERA

The period from about 1600 to 1750 is known as the Baroque era. Music, like the architecture and painting of the time, was designed on a grand scale. Several developments brought music close to its modern forms. One was the birth of opera.

"Dafne," a poem by Ottavio Rinuccini set to music by the Florentine composer Jacopo Peri, was first performed in 1597. Three years later the same artists collaborated on "Euridice." Impressed by this work, Claudio Monteverdi enlarged opera's scope and variety with his *Orfeo* of 1607, which marked the beginning of opera as it is known today. Later the Italian-born Jean-Baptiste Lully, the first major composer of ballet music, became known as the "father of French opera."

Another innovation of the Baroque period was the oratorio—a work written for solo voices, chorus, and orchestra. This had a religious subject and was presented without theatrical action. The Latin oratorios of Giacomo Carissimi were as significant as the operatic works of Monteverdi.

The Baroque age brought an increased interest in instrumental music. Keyboard instruments—including the clavichord, harpsichord, and organ—were in general use. Memorable works for these instruments were written by such composers as Domenico Scarlatti, François Couperin, and Jean-Philippe Rameau.

Stringed instruments became more popular through the innovations in design effected by the Amati family and by Antonio Stradivari, who began making violins as the Amatis' apprentice. Arcangelo Corelli gave the violin a new emphasis in the concerto grosso—music for a small group of solo instruments playing in alternation with the full orchestra. Other composers for strings were Giuseppe Tartini, notable for the Baroque solo sonata, and Antonio Vivaldi.

In the works of Henry Purcell in England, the Italian and French styles merged with the English madrigal tradition. Notable was his instrumental music and his opera *Dido and Aeneas*, first performed in 1689. There was a gradual eclipse of the old church modes upon which Western music until that time had been based. Two of them—the modes known as the Greek Ionian and Aeolian—became the major and minor scales familiar in present-day Western music.

These developments of the Baroque era culminated in the works of two giants of the time—Johann Sebastian Bach and George Frideric Handel. Both were born in Germany in 1685.

JOHANN SEBASTIAN BACH

As an organist and choirmaster for Lutheran churches near his birthplace, Bach devoted his life to composing music for the church services. His incredible output marks the summit of the polyphonic, or contrapuntal, style.

Amazingly versatile and productive, he wrote magnificent music for the organ, for choral groups, for clavier and harpsichord, for orchestra, and for small groups of instruments. Bach was the master of the technique known as the fugue. In this, voices or instrumental parts enter at different points, each imitating the first. After entering, however, each part is varied. The result is a very complex counterpoint.

Bach perfected the chorale-prelude, a contrapuntal composition based upon a chorale, or hymn tune, of the Lutheran church. Chorales were also used in Bach's cantatas. Other compositions by Bach include a number of suites, whose various movements consist of dance rhythms of the 16th to 18th centuries—the allemande, courante, saraband, and gigue.

Mozart also excelled in opera. He was the composer of such permanent favorites as *The Magic Flute*, *The Marriage of Figaro*, and *Don Giovanni*.

THE GENIUS OF BEETHOVEN

A stern individualist, Ludwig van Beethoven refused to accept the dependent position that composers before him had suffered. Although he accepted the patronage of many aristocrats, he never allowed them to dominate his work.

Beethoven was the link with a new period. His first compositions were in the Classical style. However, he soon found the old courtly forms too confining, and he burst forth with creations of a new kind. He used clashing chords—dissonance—in a way that was shocking in his day, and he initiated changes in the four movements of the symphony.

Several of Beethoven's nine symphonies are among the most famous of all musical compositions. These include the *Eroica*, which he originally called the *Bonaparte* but later renamed when he withdrew the dedication to Napoleon; the *Fifth*, which was inspired by man's struggle against fate; the *Pastoral*, which has five rather than four movements; and the noble *Choral*, which uses a chorus in the last movement. The deep and varied emotion of Beethoven is also evident in his 32 piano sonatas—including the *Moonlight, Pathétique,* and *Appassionata*—as well as in his 17 string quartets, many composed after he had become deaf.

THE ROMANTIC PERIOD

Influenced by the literature and painting of the era, 19th-century music was marked by intensely personal expressions of emotion. In order to assert their individuality with greater freedom, composers disregarded the confines of set forms. They enjoyed writing music that was more pictorial than earlier works and often attempted to imitate nature.

The new compositions often lacked the cheerfulness of the Classical era. In the quest for self-expression, composers of the Romantic period were imbued with a solemn concern for detail. Great German composers of the age were Franz Schubert and Felix Mendelssohn— sometimes called Romantic classicists—and Robert Schumann.

SCHUBERT

Although Schubert died at age 32, he wrote more than 600 songs. They represented a new kind of musical expression that he did much to perfect—the art song, or lied, in which there is perfect artistic balance between the solo voice and the piano accompaniment. The art song differs from the folk song in that it is often based upon the text of a poem and conveys subtle shades of emotion and feeling.

Schubert, a melodic genius, also wrote symphonies, chamber music, piano music, masses, and operas. His most famous symphony is the *Unfinished*.

MENDELSSOHN

A leading conductor and concert pianist as well as a composer, Mendelssohn is also noted for achieving unusual orchestral effects on the organ. He did much to revive interest in the music of Bach.

Mendelssohn's Italian and Scotch symphonies reflect the aura of these countries, and *A Midsummer Night's Dream* (which includes the "Wedding March") is equally evocative. His *Violin Concerto in E Minor* is well known, and the oratorio *Elijah* is second only to *The Messiah* in popularity.

SCHUMANN

A later exponent of the art song, Schumann wrote beautiful mood pieces and musical portraits that were also noted for their descriptive titles. In one year—1840—he composed more than 100 songs. A pianist himself, he often gave the piano accompaniment more importance than the melody.

Schumann developed his musical ideas freely and was more successful in short pieces than in longer works, which require a strong sense of structure in order to maintain continuity. There are beautiful passages, however, in his *Spring* and *Rhenish* symphonies and in his concertos.

THE FRENCH INFLUENCE

By the 1830s Paris was displacing Vienna as the world capital of musical activity. Composers flocked there to study, write, and perform.

The French stage had been revolutionized by the dramatic works of the Italian composer Luigi Cherubini, who became known as the musical czar of Paris. Cherubini—for more than 20 years the influential director of the Paris Conservatory—has been called the "link between classic idealism and modern Romanticism." In the French milieu, innovations in Romantic style and form were further developed by Hector Berlioz, Frédéric Chopin, and Franz Liszt.

BERLIOZ

A native Frenchman, Berlioz is remembered for his brilliant orchestration (the art of arranging music for the orchestra). Modern symphonic style is based on his tonal experiments, which gave woodwind, brass, and percussion instruments greater prominence.

Berlioz called his symphonies "instrumental dramas." In the *Symphonie fantastique* (the first version of which he completed and performed in 1830), Berlioz used a recurring theme, or *idée fixe* (obsession), with dramatic effect. Such a theme was a forerunner of the Wagnerian *leitmotiv* (leading theme, also called leitmotif). The composition is a good example of program music, the general term for music that tells a story or describes specific scenes or moods.

CHOPIN

Chopin was born in Poland but spent most of his adult life in Paris. A piano virtuoso, he wrote almost entirely for that instrument. To piano compositions he brought brilliant runs, a new use of widely spaced chords, and a greater use of the pedal to sustain tones and thus produce new effects.

The melodious music of Chopin conveys many emotions through the use of freer forms—for example, the nocturne, prelude, ballade, and étude. Some of his so-called salon pieces, particularly his polished waltzes, reflect the elegant life of Paris society. His mazurkas and polonaises utilize the colourful rhythms of Polish folk dances.

LISZT

A pianist even greater than Chopin, Liszt dazzled Paris and London audiences with his magnificent performances. Hungary, his native land, inspired much of his music; his popular Hungarian rhapsodies borrow from traditional Roma (Gypsy) songs.

Les Préludes, which premiered in 1854, is an example of the symphonic poem, a type of program music originated by Liszt. Later known also as a tone poem, it is often based upon a poem or a literary excerpt. It is symphonic in spirit, rather than in form.

WAGNER

One of the most illustrious of the German composers was Richard Wagner. He revolutionized opera with such spectacular works as *Lohengrin* (1850) and *Die Meistersinger* (completed in 1866). Wagner, who was his own librettist, aimed to unite upon equal terms the dramatic, musical, and visual arts. He preferred to call his works music dramas, rather than operas.

The music of Wagner was distinguished by startling innovations in chord progressions and dissonance. The way in which he used the chromatic scale—all the semitones within an octave—was later adapted and expanded by the impressionists.

A rehearsal of the first act of Wagner's opera *Siegfried* at the Théâtre du Châtelet in Paris, in 2006. Based on the Norse myth of Sigurd, Wagner conceived of the opera as depicting a new type of man who would emerge after the successful revolution for which he hoped.

Wagner's well-known anti-Jewish sentiments must be noted. The composer openly articulated his views in a number of publications, including the vitriolic *Judaism in Music* (*Das Judentum in der Musik*; 1850). For some, his anti-Semitism diminishes or even invalidates his accomplishment as a composer; for others, however, it is a personality flaw that has no bearing on his landmark status in the history of Western music. Despite the enduring controversy over his religious and political views, Wagner's works have been performed by both Jewish and non-Jewish musicians since the 19th century. Whether inconsequential or a detriment to his artistic legacy, Wagner's anti-Semitism and its role in his musical production will likely remain a matter of dispute.

BRAHMS

With Wagner and Beethoven, Johannes Brahms dominated the music of the 19th century. He retained the formal lines of the sonata and the symphony, as developed by the classicists, yet reflected the Romantic spirit too, infusing his work with deep feeling.

When Brahms completed his first symphony, the noted conductor-critic Hans von Bülow called it the Tenth—a successor to Beethoven's nine symphonies. Von Bülow also originated the familiar catchphrase the "three B's"—for Bach, Beethoven, and Brahms. In addition to four symphonies, Brahms composed art songs, Romantic pieces for the piano, chamber music, and concertos for piano and violin.

OPERA IN THE 19TH CENTURY

Many of the greatest operas of all time were composed during the 19th century. In the early 1800s Italian opera was enriched by

Gioacchino Rossini, Gaetano Donizetti, and Vincenzo Bellini. They were followed by Pietro Mascagni, Ruggiero Leoncavallo, Giacomo Puccini, and the unsurpassed Giuseppe Verdi. French opera benefited from the talents of Jacques Halévy, Giacomo Meyerbeer, Charles Gounod, Jules Massenet, and Georges Bizet.

The lighthearted opéra bouffe of Jacques Offenbach in France led to the enduring comic operas of the collaborators Arthur Sullivan and William S. Gilbert in England. Light opera, or operetta, in the United States began with the popular productions of Victor Herbert.

LATE ROMANTICS

In the last half of the 19th century, several composers were continuing in the Romantic tradition. The art song received fresh treatment by Hugo Wolf, a composer with a wealth of melodic ideas depicting mood,

Richard Strauss in 1934, at work on his new opera, *Die Schweigsame Frau* (*The Silent Woman*)

character, and situation. Anton Bruckner and Gustav Mahler composed large-scale dramatic symphonies that utilized harmonic innovations and expanded orchestras.

Richard Strauss followed the path blazed by Wagner. Like Wagner, he was a master of orchestration and showed a strong sense of realism. He composed the symphonic poem *Till Eulenspiegel's Merry Pranks* (1894–95) and the opera *Der Rosenkavalier* (1909–1910).

Meanwhile, the Russian pianist-composer Sergey Rachmaninoff was the Romantic successor of Chopin and Liszt. He was renowned for such piano concertos as *Prelude in C Sharp Minor*, played for the first time in public on September 26, 1892.

CLASSICAL MUSIC IN THE 20TH CENTURY

By the turn of the 20th century, musical works were becoming more widely known through technological advances. Composers were searching for new kinds of musical expression.

Just as painters had turned from Realism to Impressionism, composers began to write in a more subtle style. This new style was a reaction against the emotional excesses of the Romantic school.

THE FIRST MODERNISTS

The first composer to be called an Impressionist was a Frenchman, Claude Debussy. Debussy used shifting harmonies, based on the whole-tone scale, to give listeners an impression, rather than a clear visualization, of what they were hearing—as in his cycle of *Nocturnes* for orchestra.

Igor Stravinsky was born in Russia. After achieving renown in France, he moved to the United States. Originally a composer of ballet music, he aroused storms of protest with *The Rite of Spring*, first performed in Paris in 1913. He made daring experiments with harmony and drew on a wide knowledge of music of all kinds for his effects.

Another controversial composer was Arnold Schoenberg. Trained in the Romantic school, he abandoned existing scales in favor of the 12-tone series, previously used only in short passages. This system, which permitted a freer use of harmony, was also used by two pupils of Schoenberg—Alban Berg, celebrated for his opera *Wozzeck* (1925), and Anton von Webern.

Béla Bartók, a Hungarian steeped in the folk tunes of his native country, used this music and other sources for experiments in dissonance. Zoltán Kodály, another composer who drew on a Hungarian background, showed a strong lyric and melodic sense.

OTHER 20TH-CENTURY COMPOSERS

Modernism was fused with the spirit of the Classical period in the compositions of German-born Paul Hindemith. He made use of atonality, but his work showed a dependence upon the strict forms of Bach and Mozart and was referred to as neoclassic.

In Britain, Ralph Vaughan Williams used English folk music as a basis for his works, which include *A Sea Symphony* and *Pastoral Symphony.* He and Sir Edward Elgar, who wrote *Pomp and Circumstance*, were the most representative English composers after Purcell. Of a later generation, Benjamin Britten showed a gift for setting an appropriate mood without departing from the simplest structure.

Sergei Prokofiev blended modernism, classicism, and Russian nationalism in his many compositions. His *Peter and the Wolf* has acquainted generations of children with the instrumentation of the orchestra through its use of individual instruments and distinctive themes to identify each character.

Despite the handicap of writing music acceptable to the Soviet Union's Communist regime, such talents as Dmitri Shostakovich and Aram Khachaturian flourished. Several of Shostakovich's symphonies are considered masterpieces; Khachaturian's *Gayne* ballet suite produced a popular song—"The Saber Dance."

A new genre of nationalism emerged with the creation of Latin American classical music. Mexican composers included Carlos Chávez (*Sinfonia India*) and Silvestre Revueltas (*Sensemayá*). Afro-Cuban folk music inspired Cuba's Ernesto Lecuona (*Malagueña*). Alberto Ginastera of Argentina used folk elements in orchestral, ballet, and chamber music. The most prolific Latin American composer was Brazil's Heitor Villa-Lobos (*Bachianas Brasileiras*).

After World War II a new school of post-Schoenberg serialism (based on the 12-tone series) developed, with Stravinsky reflecting the change. His *Threni* (1958) and *Movements for Piano and Orchestra* (1960) used a freer approach to the row order, and his musical textures became more sparse.

Beginning in the 1980s, melody—of a uniquely 20th-century kind—reasserted itself among composers. The minimalist composers—Americans Steve Reich, Philip Glass, and John Adams—formed one group. Their main influences were the simple harmonic and highly repetitive melodic patterns of the music of India, Bali, and West Africa. Another type of melody was represented by the intense atmospherics of Witold Lutoslawski of Poland and Peter Maxwell Davies and Michael Tippett of England.

Electronic music, as opposed to music played on electronic instruments, began in 1948 with Pierre Schaeffer in Paris. Called *musique concrète,* it used natural sounds that were recorded on tape and then combined and altered or distorted to form a unified artistic whole. The 10-movement *Symphony for One Man Only,* composed by Schaeffer and his collaborator, Pierre Henry, in 1949–50, is a landmark in the development of tape music.

When the music synthesizer was introduced in 1955 in Princeton, N.J., it made virtually every kind of sound or combination of sounds available to the composer. Babbitt was an early exponent of the instrument with his *Composition for Synthesizer* in 1961.

The next step was the computer. An early example of computer music was *Illiac Suite* for string quartet, which was "composed" by the Illiac digital computer at the University of Illinois in 1957. The computer was programmed to generate random integers that represented pitches and note values. The integers were then screened by instructions based on traditional rules of composition. A further development in 1963, engineered by Max V. Mathews at the Bell Telephone Laboratories, was the direct synthesis of sound programmed by a deck of punched cards. This eliminated the need for a performer.

COUNTRY MUSIC

Country music is a form of American popular music that originated in the rural South and

West. It is sometimes called country and western. The longtime center of country music is Nashville, Tennessee, though the style has a national and international following.

Country music is an offshoot of the folk music brought to the Appalachians and to other parts of the American South by English, Scottish, and Irish settlers of the 1700s and 1800s. This music changed as it came in contact with ethnic musics of other immigrants—Acadian (Cajun) in Louisiana, Latin in the Southwest, African throughout much of the South—and other musical genres such as blues and gospel. This intermingling of styles was the birth of country music.

In the early 1920s, radio stations began broadcasting shows called barn dances, modeled after the informal social dancing of the American frontier. WSM in Nashville began broadcasting its "WSM Barn Dance"— the future Grand Ole Opry—in 1925. Record companies discovered the commercial possibilities of this music, and Georgia fiddler John Carson had the first sales success with his recording of "Little Old Log Cabin in the Lane" in 1923. In 1927 singer Jimmie Rodgers, originally a yodeler, made his first recordings. Because Rodgers inspired numerous performers to become country entertainers, he became known as the "Father of Country

Music." The other highly influential act to emerge at this time was the Carter Family. Early recordings were of ballads and country dance tunes and featured mainly fiddle, guitar, and banjo.

During the 1930s a number of "singing cowboy" film stars greatly expanded the audience for country music. These singers and actors—the most famous being Gene Autry and Roy Rogers—performed songs about an idealized American West. Their success helped to popularize the term "country and western music" as a replacement for the earlier label "hillbilly music," which many performers found offensive.

The migration of many southern rural whites to industrial cities during the Great Depression and World War II accelerated country music's growth away from an exclusively southern and rural phenomenon. Bob Wills popularized a style of country music called western swing, which drew from such influences as the swing jazz of African American orchestras and featured amplified guitars and a strong dance rhythm. The style called honky-tonk emerged in the 1940s and featured fiddle and steel guitar paired with sentimental lyrics of hard-luck stories. Ernest Tubb and Hank Williams were famous honky-tonk stars of the day.

In the same period some artists returned to country music's roots. Mandolin player Bill

Roy Acuff, fiddle at the ready, celebrates 54 years with the Grand Ole Opry in Nashville, Tenn., on June 15, 1992.

Monroe and his string band, the Blue Grass Boys, featured traditional instrumentation and high harmony singing. Their music became known as bluegrass, after the name of their band.

In the postwar years country music found unprecedented popular appeal. In 1942 Roy Acuff, one of the most important country singers, had co-organized the first publishing house for country music in Nashville, which soon became the home of the country music industry. There, the Grand Ole Opry emerged as the top performance venue, and recording and music publishing companies opened offices.

In the 1950s and '60s country music became a huge commercial enterprise, with such leading performers as Tex Ritter, Johnny Cash, Buck Owens, Merle Haggard, and Charley Pride. Patsy Cline, Tammy Wynette, Jim Reeves, Eddy Arnold, and others popularized a style known as the Nashville sound, which featured smooth arrangements emphasizing string sections and background vocalists. Television boosted the fortunes of country music generally and such artists as Porter Wagoner, Jimmy Dean, Loretta Lynn, and Dolly Parton in particular.

Country music has a long history of broadening its audience by adapting stylistic elements—both vocal and instrumental— of rock and other popular music. In part a response to the Nashville sound, Willie Nelson, Waylon Jennings, and other stars introduced in the 1970s a new style called "outlaw" country, which was inspired by rock music. The crossover phenomenon came to the fore in the late 1970s and early '80s, when such pop-country stars as Kenny Rogers, Alabama, and the Oak Ridge Boys attained success with younger, urban pop-music fans. Crossover performers who blended country with rock and pop in the 1990s and 2000s included Garth Brooks, Faith Hill, Shania Twain, the Dixie Chicks, Carrie Underwood, Taylor Swift, and Rascal Flatts.

Taylor Swift performs at the 2014 iHeartRadio Music Festival at the MGM Grand Garden Arena in Las Vegas, Nev., on Sept. 19, 2014.

While crossover artists and country music innovators expanded the definition of country music, the appeal of country music's traditions persisted. In the 1980s and 1990s the "new traditionalist" movement arose among artists who adhered to the classic country sound, style, and themes. Among them were Ricky Skaggs, George Strait, Reba McEntire, Randy Travis, the Judds, Dwight Yoakam, Alan Jackson, and Lee Ann Womack.

SWINGING AND BOPPING INTO JAZZ

In the early decades of the 20th century, the word "jazz" was used to mean most kinds of American popular and dance music. Since the 1920s, however, jazz has usually signified a tradition in black American music that began as a folk music in the South and developed gradually into a sophisticated modern art. While classical and rock music have often borrowed features of jazz, they remain outside the jazz tradition.

Unique features of jazz are its sounds and its rhythms. As a basically improvised kind of music, jazz's goal has always been to express strongly felt emotions. So jazz improvisers adapted standard band and orchestra instruments such as the trumpet and trombone to their expressive purposes. They also rediscovered neglected or forgotten instruments such as the saxophone. Instruments such as the violin, tuba, and flute have been used much less often because they are less able to express the feelings of jazz. Jazz features syncopated rhythms—rhythms with stimulating, offbeat accents. The several instruments in jazz groups are usually played in separate rhythms that unite to create an uplifting effect.

The jazz improviser creates and plays music simultaneously, unlike the composer who creates music at leisure and may never perform it. The improvised jazz solo may be variations on a theme, or it may consist of entirely new melodies. In either kind of solo, the player tries to create natural, flowing melodies. A solo, say jazz musicians, should "tell a little story." Typically jazz band compositions and arrangements leave many spaces for improvisation.

BEGINNINGS

The first jazz was played in the early 20th century. The work chants, spirituals, and folk music of black Americans are among the sources of jazz, which reflects the rhythms and expressions of West African song. The earliest jazz musicians also drew upon marches, opera arias, popular songs, ragtime, and blues for their inspiration.

SCOTT JOPLIN

A black composer and pianist, Scott Joplin has been known as the King of Ragtime since the turn of the 20th century. His classic ragtime pieces for the piano—including "Maple Leaf Rag" and "The Entertainer," published from 1899 through 1909—made him famous. Musicians continued to perform his music for decades after his death, and interest in Joplin and ragtime was renewed in the 1970s with the use of his music in the Academy Award-winning score for the movie *The Sting*.

Scott Joplin was born in Bowie (now Texarkana), Texas, on November 24, 1868. From the mid-1880s, he traveled through the Midwest, performing at the World's Columbian Exposition in Chicago in 1893. In 1895 he settled in Sedalia, Missouri, where he studied music at the George R. Smith College for Negroes.

Joplin's first published extended work was a ballet suite (1902), using all the rhythmic devices of ragtime. In 1907 he moved to New York City and wrote an instruction book, *The School of Ragtime*, which outlined his complex bass patterns, syncopation and breaks, and harmonic ideas. He published his opera *Treemonisha* in 1911 at his own expense. This work combined all his musical ideas into a conventional, three-act opera. He became obsessed with producing the opera, and the obsession drove him to a nervous breakdown. He was institutionalized in 1916, and he died on April 1, 1917, in New York City.

Ragtime, a black American music that first appeared in the 1890s, was composed for the piano, and each rag is a composition with several themes. The leading ragtime composer was Scott Joplin. Originally a blues was a song of sorrow, sung slowly to the accompaniment of piano or guitar. A blues is 12 measures long, and typically the first line is repeated. For example, "The blue sky is my blanket, and the moonlight is my spread, Blue sky is my blanket, and the moonlight is my spread, A rock is my pillow, that's where I lay my head."

EARLY JAZZ

According to legend, the first improvising jazz musician was the cornetist Buddy Bolden, leader of a band in New Orleans. The first jazz bands were usually made up of one or two cornet players who played the principal melodies, a clarinetist and trombonist who

BESSIE SMITH

One of the greatest of the blues singers, Bessie Smith sang of the cares and troubles she had known—of poverty and oppression, of love and indifference. Her art is known today through the more than 150 songs she recorded during her brief career.

Bessie Smith was born on April 15, probably in 1894, in Chattanooga, Tennessee. Her family was poor, and she got her start as a singer with the help of Ma Rainey, one of the first great professional blues vocalists. Rainey organized troupes of musicians and dancers and led them on tours of the South and the Midwest.

Smith was discovered by a record company representative—the pianist and composer Clarence Williams. She made her first recordings— "Down Hearted Blues" and "Gulf Coast Blues"—in February 1923. These sold very well, and by the end of 1925 she had made a number of successful recordings, some of them accompanied by the trumpet playing of the legendary Louis Armstrong.

Smith's great popularity continued through the 1920s, and in 1929 she made a short motion picture, *Saint Louis Blues*. Then, with the 1930s and the Great Depression, public taste began to change. The blues lost some of their appeal, and blues recordings did not sell very well. Smith continued singing, appearing at clubs in Philadelphia and New York City and varying her act by introducing popular songs among the blues numbers. She also became increasingly dependent on alcohol, which made it more difficult for her to find work. While traveling in Mississippi, Smith was seriously injured in an automobile accident. She died on Sept. 26, 1937, while being taken to the hospital in Clarksdale, Mississippi.

Smith's recordings, which have been collected into albums, remain popular. Her work influenced a number of successful singers, including **Billie Holiday, Mahalia Jackson, and Janis Joplin.**

Bessie Smith strikes a pose in New York City circa 1925.

improvised countermelodies, and a rhythm section (piano, banjo, string bass or tuba, and drums) to accompany the horns. These bands played for dancers or marched in parades in the warm southern climate.

Some of the first New Orleans musicians were among the most stirring of all jazz artists. They include clarinetist Johnny Dodds, clarinetist-soprano saxophonist Sidney Bechet, pianist Jelly Roll Morton, and cornetist King Oliver. The first jazz record was made in 1917 by a New Orleans band—the Original Dixieland Jass Band, made up of white musicians who copied black styles.

The New Orleans musicians discovered that audiences were eager for their music in the cities of the North and the Midwest. In the 1920s Chicago became the second major jazz center—the new home for Morton and Oliver, among others. White Chicago youths, such as tenor saxophonist Bud Freeman and clarinetist Benny Goodman, were excited by the New Orleans masters—including the thrilling Louis Armstrong, who played in King Oliver's band—and formed their own Dixieland jazz bands. Pee Wee Russell (clarinet), Jack Teagarden (trombone), and the gifted melodic cornetist Bix Beiderbecke went to Chicago to help create this new hot jazz.

The third major jazz center was New York City, and it became the most important. In New York, pianists such as James P. Johnson created the "stride" piano style by transforming rags and southern black folk dances into jazz. Big band jazz was first played in the ballrooms and theatres of New York. The cornets, clarinets, and trombones of Dixieland became trumpet sections, saxophone sections, and trombone sections in Fletcher Henderson's ensemble. Big band jazz was smoother, with lighter rhythms, but no less exciting than Dixieland.

The New Orleans trumpeter who became a world ambassador for jazz, Louis Armstrong learned to blow on a bugle in reform school when he was 13.

SWING ERA

Louis Armstrong was the first great jazz soloist. He played vividly dramatic cornet and trumpet solos with his Hot Five and Hot Seven from 1925 to 1928 and then with a series of big bands. His rhythmic feeling was a rare combination of tension and relaxation that inspired the word "swing." The free, loose feeling of music that swings

BENNY GOODMAN

At the height of the swing era, the King of Swing was American clarinetist and bandleader Benny Goodman. It was Goodman's orchestra that established the most popular big-band jazz style of the 1930s and brought a new level of recognition to jazz. Along with recording a string of hit songs, he also introduced several other top jazz and popular music performers.

Benjamin David Goodman was born on May 30, 1909, in Chicago. The son of Russian Jewish immigrants, he received his first music training in 1919 at a Chicago synagogue, and the following year he played in bands and took lessons at Jane Addams's Hull House. He studied with German classical instructor Franz Schoepp and absorbed jazz basics through jam sessions with Chicago-area musicians. In 1926 Goodman joined the Ben Pollack jazz band and made his first solo recording, "He's the Last Word." He lived in New York City from 1929 and worked as a studio musician, performing on more than 1,000 recordings. In 1933–34 he formed his own big band that played regularly on *Let's Dance*, a late-night network radio program.

In May 1935, Goodman took his band on a tour of the United States that was a failure until he reached the Palomar Ballroom in Los Angeles in August. There, crowds of enthusiastic young dancers and fans of *Let's Dance* greeted the band, and the swing era in popular music began.

From this point, the Goodman band went on to unprecedented heights of fame. The band's hits during its early years included "Don't Be That Way," "Stompin' at the Savoy," and "Goody Goody," as well as the band's two theme songs "Let's Dance" and "Goodbye." The group became a favorite of white audiences while playing orchestrations by outstanding black arrangers, especially Fletcher Henderson. Goodman also pioneered racial integration in his jazz trio (1935–36), quartet (1936–39), and sextet (1939–41), featuring black musicians, including Teddy Wilson (piano), Lionel Hampton (vibraphone), and Charlie Christian (guitar). Band members Harry James (trumpet) and Gene Krupa (drums) and singer Peggy Lee also rose to fame while working with Goodman. In pioneering the small group, or chamber jazz ensemble, Goodman made what is perhaps his most important contribution to jazz history.

(continued on the next page)

(continued from the previous page)

The Goodman orchestra performed at Carnegie Hall in New York City with guest artists from the bands of Duke Ellington and Count Basie in January 1938. The recording of the highly successful evening has been released several times and is heralded as one of the greatest albums of live jazz. Goodman reorganized his band in the 1940s and brought in new talent and arrangers, including Eddie Sauter and Mel Powell, who took the band in a more modern direction. As the 1940s progressed, the bop movement began to replace swing music, and Goodman broke up his band. He intermittently led small and big bands during the 1950s and recorded in the traditional, classical swing style. In 1955 he recorded the soundtrack for *The Benny Goodman Story*, a movie loosely based on his life. In 1962 he took a jazz band to the Soviet Union on a U.S. State Department tour. He went on to appear occasionally in special concerts, on world tours, and as a clarinetist with symphonic orchestras and smaller groups. Goodman died on June 13, 1986, in New York City.

became the major feature of the swing era, which lasted from about 1930 to 1945. Radio popularized the sounds of swing bands.

"It don't mean a thing (if it ain't got that swing)," according to a 1932 Duke Ellington piece of the same title. Ellington composed music full of colourful sounds and imaginative melodies. The soloists in his big band were very individualistic, playing clarinet cries, saxophone moans, and trumpet growls to his hundreds of compositions.

Again and again Ellington portrayed black life in the U.S. in song suites such as "My People and Black, Brown and Beige" and in short masterpieces such as "Main Stem" and "Mood Indigo." Ellington's career lasted for over a half century. In the 1960s he began performing his original concerts of sacred music in churches in the United States and Europe.

BOP ERA

Bop blossomed out of informal performances—jam sessions—in New York City's Harlem in the early 1940s. Among these new musicians, Charlie Parker was the leading personality. His exciting alto saxophone flights won him the popular nickname of Bird, yet he played equally creatively in ballads and in heartfelt blues such as "Parker's Mood." His broken melodies were rich with surprising accents and highly contrasted rhythms. Bop required extremely fine, indeed almost virtuoso, technique to play, and Parker was the most skillful of all bop musicians.

Many bop pieces were played at the fastest tempos yet heard in jazz. Bop featured many-noted solos and unusual, quickly changing harmonies; also, bop drummers began playing startling accents, "dropping bombs" on bass drums. Dizzy Gillespie and Fats Navarro played soaring high notes on their trumpets, while Bud Powell created long, uninterrupted streams of piano melody. Even though bop was difficult to sing, a few vocalists such as Sarah Vaughan had the necessary control and wide voice range.

The bop era, which lasted from about 1945 to 1960, was also the period of cool jazz. This was a music that offered the harmonic discoveries of bop while avoiding bop's most irregular rhythms. The leaders of the cool jazz movement were piano player Lennie Tristano, who believed in completely spontaneous improvisation, and his students Lee Konitz and Warne Marsh, who both played saxophones. The white West Coast musicians of the 1950s were inspired by cool jazz to create a soft, quiet kind of improvisation. Among them Art Pepper was most unusual for his boldness and for the strong emotional quality of his alto saxophone improvising.

The opposite of cool jazz was hard bop, which was played in the eastern cities. Hard bop was vigorous and energetic and emphasized the black American basis of jazz. Hard bop songs were enriched by the soulful harmonies of blues and black church music, and as a result the electronic organ became a popular jazz instrument. Like bop, hard bop was played not by big bands but by small instrumental groups. Hard bop composers such as the prolific Horace Silver wrote arrangements that attempted to make five musicians sound as powerful as an 18-piece big band. The aggressiveness of Silver's quintets was matched by the quintet headed by Clifford Brown on trumpet and Max Roach on drums. Art Blakey played powerful drum syncopations, inflaming the players in successive groups of his Jazz Messengers.

Many swing and bop musicians rejected pianist Thelonious Monk because of his harsh, zigzagging melodies and startling blues discords. Yet Monk was respected for the songs he composed, many of which were played by virtually all 1950s musicians: "Round Midnight," "Blue Monk," and "Rhythm-a-ning." And some musicians understood Monk's subtle style of improvising. Sonny Rollins was a forceful, dramatic tenor saxophonist who was originally inspired by Parker, Hawkins, and Young, the greatest swing and bop saxophonists. He became Monk's student and featured a cruel, Monk-like sense of humor and sudden, breathtaking melodies.

There was one musician who played in almost every possible kind of bop era ensemble—Miles Davis. When Davis was 19, he became trumpeter in one of Parker's bop groups. Then Davis led one of the first cool jazz groups and began leading a quintet of hard bop musicians in the 1950s. Sometimes Davis's trumpet playing was fast and angry; often it was lonely and haunting, in echoes of the sound of Spanish folk music. Davis liked to play pieces in which the basic patterns of harmony remained unchanging for long periods of time. This kind of harmonic structure was called "modal." Much of the new jazz of the 1960s was based on modal structures.

The 1950s also brought forth composers who were not considered either bop or hard bop creators. The popular Modern Jazz Quartet offered the delicate, almost cool, compositions of its pianist, John Lewis. In contrast Herbie Nichols was neglected until after his death in 1963 and only recorded a few albums of his many sharp-witted, brisk piano portraits. The traditional forms of jazz songs were abandoned by Lewis, Nichols, and George Russell, who wrote complex, brightly colourful works for big bands. Written themes were only a small part of Charles Mingus's compositions. He built instead grand, highly emotional pieces out of blocks of music by mixing his soloists, rhythms, accompaniments, and sound colours.

MODERN ERA

"I believe music is really a free thing," said alto saxophonist Ornette Coleman, who abandoned the harmonic structures of the bop era. His music was emotionally impulsive. Often the sound of his saxophone changed from one phrase to the next as he played in and out of tune with completely unpredictable accents. Bop and swing musicians thought Coleman's music was impossibly discordant and difficult. For his *Free Jazz* album (1960) a double quartet of musicians improvised in turn, each supporting or inspiring the others.

Coleman's excitingly expressive style influenced Eric Dolphy and John Coltrane. One of the free jazz improvisers, Dolphy imitated birdcalls on his flute, played wild, fast, lurching alto saxophone solos, and made his bass clarinet sound like people talking. (Free jazz is a movement that began in the late 1950s wherein performers use random improvisation, straying far from traditional jazz harmonies and forms.) For Coltrane's 37-minute album *Ascension* the free-blowing ensemble work of seven horn players, backed by a rhythm quartet, alternates with their searing solo passages. Coltrane played long tenor saxophone solos that began with hard bop phrases and moved to harsh, guttural sounds and high screams.

With his piano, electronic organ, and synthesizer, the mystic Sun Ra led his Arkestra of space-suited musicians on imaginary journeys to distant stars. Cecil Taylor's piano music was the most complex jazz of all. His long solos were constructed in near-symphonic fashion, with many themes and many rhythms building to grand climaxes at tornado-fast tempos. Like Taylor, tenor saxophonist Albert Ayler believed emotional excitement was more important than melody. Ayler's songs began as simple marches but turned into extremely discordant honking, wailing, and screaming at the fastest possible tempos.

Chicago revived as a jazz center in 1965 when a cooperative, the Association for the Advancement of Creative Musicians (AACM), was formed to produce concerts and to teach music to inner-city youths. Founded by Muhal Richard Abrams, it generated Anthony Braxton's and Henry Threadgill's groups and the Art Ensemble of Chicago. AACM artists played hundreds of instruments, many of which had never been used in jazz before. These included bells, sirens, whistles, musical toys, African drums, and instruments that they built themselves.

European enthusiasm about post-1960 jazz led to two important trends of the 1970s and 1980s. First, improvising musicians from many countries were inspired to draw on their individual musical heritages to create new kinds of jazz. Second, American jazz musicians—for example, Don Cherry, master of the pocket trumpet—discovered ways of joining black musical traditions with musics from around the world. The most popular result of this trend to variety has been fusion music, which joins jazz, rock, and Latin-American rhythms.

RHYTHM AND BLUES

Coined by music journalist Jerry Wexler in 1947, the term "rhythm and blues," or "R&B," has been applied to a number of different types of popular black music. It originally described an urban music style that grew out of the blues in the period after World War II. Today the term is most commonly used for music that is more closely related to soul and hip-hop than to that of the early R&B pioneers.

The closest forerunner of rhythm and blues was a style of blues popularized in the 1930s by bandleader Louis Jordan. This music, sometimes called jump blues, was characterized by humorous lyrics and upbeat rhythms derived from the piano-based boogie-woogie blues style as well as classic blues. Some performers added jazz and even Latin influences to the mix. Along

with Jordan, some of the
leading artists in this style
were Amos Milburn, Roy
Milton, Jimmy Liggins,
Joe Liggins, Floyd Dixon,
Wynonie Harris, Big Joe
Turner, and Charles Brown.

Early rhythm and
blues was recorded
largely in Los Angeles by
small record labels such
as Modern, RPM, and
Specialty. The founding
of Atlantic Records in
1947 by Ahmet Ertegun
and Herb Abramson
shifted the industry's
center to New York City.
In 1953 they brought
in Wexler as a partner,
and he and Ertegun
were instrumental in
moving rhythm-and-blues
music forward. Atlantic
hired jazz musicians as
studio players and paid
particular attention to
the sound quality of their
recordings. The label
introduced some of the
top female names in
rhythm and blues—most

was accompanied by the popularity of such folksingers as Pete Seeger and the pure-voiced soprano Joan Baez. Other acts, such as Peter, Paul and Mary, created a bridge between traditional folk music and rock. The intersection of the folk tradition and rock came to be known as folk rock. The genre offered socially conscious rock music flavoured by such traditional music as English and Celtic ballads and gospel songs. Popular folk-rock acts included the Mamas and the Papas, Simon and Garfunkel, and the Byrds.

The pivotal artist in the fusion of folk and rock, and the one whose music reflected social changes most dramatically, was Bob Dylan. He began as a folksinger in the early 1960s and soon began writing songs urging peace ("A Hard Rain's A-Gonna Fall") and equal rights for all Americans ("Blowin' in the Wind"). In 1965 he began leading

The Beach Boys are shown in the mid-1960s. Brian Wilson is the tall one in the back.

rock bands. His songs then became more personal and abstract, with complex, poetic lyrics unprecedented in popular music.

SURF ROCK

As surfing became popular in the United States in the early 1960s, a new genre of rock emerged to represent the West Coast lifestyle. Surf rock's characteristic cascading electric-guitar playing was developed by surfer Dick Dale and his band the Del-Tones. The Beach Boys were the best-known act of the surf genre. Led by Brian Wilson, the band at first sang songs about surfing and "California Girls" in sweet barbershop quartet harmonies. By the mid-1960s they became interested in new recording-studio technologies such as overdubbing—a technique of recording engineering that made their five voices sound like many more—in complex harmonies such as those of "Good Vibrations."

THE BRITISH INVASION

In the 1950s rock and roll in Britain was predominantly imported from the United States. By the early 1960s, however, British youth weaned on American blues, rhythm and blues, and rock had developed a vital rock scene of their own. Soon rock swept across the Atlantic once again, this time from Britain to the United States in a movement called the British Invasion.

The defining band of the British Invasion was the Beatles. A quartet of musicians from Liverpool, England—John Lennon, Paul McCartney, George Harrison, and Ringo Starr—the Beatles were already a phenomenon in Britain before arriving triumphantly in New York City in early 1964. They sang songs written mainly by Lennon and McCartney, whose infectious music and witty lyrics made them two of the finest 20th-century songwriters. Early Beatles songs were in standard forms ("She Loves You"). Their lyrics gradually became more subtle and tender ("Yesterday") and sometimes abstract ("A Day in the Life"). Leading rock music experimenters, the Beatles often used overdubbing and other advanced record-production techniques to invent new musical effects. They disbanded in 1970.

THE BEATLES

The Beatles generated a phenomenal run of gold records that endured long after the rock group disbanded. Affectionately nicknamed the Fab Four, the band's fresh-faced appeal inspired a worldwide frenzy of fandom in the 1960s called Beatlemania. Their music, rooted in American rock and roll but liberally flavoured with rhythm and blues and rockabilly, featured harmonic vocals, melodic guitar, and a driving backbeat that influenced scores of young musicians and revolutionized popular music. As musicians, as composers, and as entertainers, the Beatles bridged generation gaps and language barriers, reshaping rock music with their wit and sophistication. As trendsetters of youth counterculture, they popularized long hair, mod dress, hallucinogenic drugs, Indian music, and Eastern mysticism.

The three guitarists in the group—John Lennon (Oct. 9, 1940–Dec. 8, 1980), Paul McCartney (born June 18, 1942), and George Harrison (Feb. 25, 1943–Nov. 29, 2001)—first played together as schoolboys in the late 1950s with a band named the Quarrymen. The group was renamed Johnny and the Moondogs, the Moonshiners, then the Silver Beatles (a wordplay on the musical term "beat" that also paid tribute to rocker Buddy Holly's Crickets). Drummer Pete Best (born Nov. 24, 1941) joined the band in 1960, and Stu Sutcliffe (June 23, 1940–April 10, 1962) played bass for them for several months that year. After Sutcliffe left the band, McCartney switched to playing bass. (Sutcliffe was to die in 1962 from a brain hemorrhage.)

The band performed regularly in Liverpool as well as Hamburg, Germany. In Liverpool, they became a regular fixture at the Cavern Club, where they caught the attention of local record-shop owner Brian Epstein, who

The Beatles perform on *The Ed Sullivan Show* on Feb. 9, 1964. In the foreground (*left to right*) are Paul McCartney, George Harrison, and John Lennon; Ringo Starr plays the drums.

offered to manage the band. Epstein had the group shed its leather jackets for more respectable suit jackets and ties. In 1962 the band—now known as simply the Beatles—fired Best and replaced him with another Liverpool drummer, Ringo Starr (byname of Richard Starkey; born July 7, 1940). Epstein secured a recording contract for the band and convinced record producer George Martin to produce the first songs of the Lennon and McCartney songwriting team.

Most of the Beatles' early recordings feature fairly straightforward pop love songs. Their first record—a Lennon-McCartney song called "Love Me Do"—was released in October 1962 and became an immediate hit. By the time they led the so-called British invasion of the United States in 1964, the band held the top five spots on the singles recording charts and had released their first film, *A Hard Day's Night*. Within a year, six of their albums in succession hit the top of the charts, and *Help!*, another antic musical film, opened to critical acclaim. By then, the frenzy that came to be called Beatlemania was a global phenomenon.

For all the Beatles' success, however, there were also controversial incidents, such as the group's rebuff of an invitation to a meeting with leaders of the Philippines and Lennon's remark to a reporter that the Beatles were more popular than Jesus Christ. While Lennon apologized for his statement, he continued to cause controversy in the years to come. By 1966, the strain of constant touring coupled with the pressure of being the world's most popular musicians had taken its toll, and the band announced their retirement from live performances, stating that they would focus on studio work.

In 1967 the Beatles released *Sgt. Pepper's Lonely Hearts Club Band.* The album demonstrated the group's dramatic evolution in music and personal appearance. The Beatles' songs featured complex orchestration and cryptic lyrics, while their formerly clean-shaven faces sported moustaches.

The later Beatles albums were like variety shows—a miscellany of rock, blues, country, folk, ballads, social commentary, nursery rhymes, 1920s parodies, and satires of other pop groups, with an occasional injection of surrealism. Most of their material was credited to Lennon and McCartney as a team; in time Lennon's sardonic songs were recognizable because they were generally composed in the first person, while McCartney's songs developed scenarios with offbeat characters. In addition to the landmark *Sgt. Pepper's* album, their most acclaimed works were the innovative *Revolver* (1966); the exuberant *The Beatles* (1968), commonly referred to as the "White Album"; and their last joint effort, *Abbey Road* (1969). (*Let It Be*, issued in 1970, had been delayed for simultaneous release with a film and book.)

Amid public quarrels and lawsuits, the Beatles officially broke up in 1970. Lennon had begun recording with his second wife, the avant-garde conceptual artist Yoko Ono, and McCartney formed the successful soft-rock group Wings with his wife, Linda. Harrison and Starr also recorded solo albums.

Rumors that the Beatles would reunite persisted for a decade after the band's demise until Lennon was murdered in New York City in 1980. In 1995 an anthology of the band's recordings was released alongside a video catalog of their history together. Harrison, McCartney, and Starr reunited to issue two new recordings for the project from previously unrecorded material. Using state-of-the-art recording technology, the voice of John Lennon was incorporated into the tracks. Although the public camaraderie of the three surviving Beatles following the project ignited hopes for a reunion tour, the musicians made clear their decision to leave the past in the past. With Harrison's death in 2001 after a battle with cancer, the hope of a reunion tour was finally laid to rest.

Two other seminal bands of the era, the Rolling Stones and the Who, were counterpoints to the Beatles. In contrast to the Beatles' respectability and charm, the Stones cultivated a rebellious image and played brash, often dark music to match. Successful recording artists, the Stones were also great concert performers, propelled by the energy of lead singer Mick Jagger and the intensity of guitarist Keith Richards. The Who shunned Beatlesque love songs in favor of aggressive songs of teenage angst. Their legendarily loud concerts ended with them smashing their instruments onstage. In 1969 the Who originated the rock opera with *Tommy*. Both the Rolling Stones and the Beatles proved to be among rock's most durable bands, with members still performing five decades after their 1960s debuts.

PSYCHEDELIC ROCK

The hippie counterculture of the 1960s gave rise to a genre called psychedelic, or "acid," rock. It featured song lyrics about psychedelic drugs and incorporated feedback and distortion, improvisation, and long instrumental solos.

Guitarist Jimi Hendrix, the gravel-voiced singer Janis Joplin, the Jefferson Airplane, the Doors, and the Grateful Dead were the most prominent of psychedelic rock performers. Hendrix created masterly solos using extremely loud volumes and creative sound effects. He ended his shows by setting fire to his guitar. Joplin and Hendrix died of drug overdoses within a month of each other in 1970, both at age 27. The gifted lead singer of the Doors, Jim Morrison, died a year later at the same young age. Despite the short lives of most psychedelic bands (the Grateful Dead being a notable exception), the genre had a huge impact on rock music, greatly influencing such offshoots as heavy metal, progressive and art rock, funk, punk, and electronic music.

ART ROCK

An eclectic branch of rock music that emerged in the late 1960s and flourished in the early to mid-1970s, art rock is sometimes used synonymously with progressive rock, but the latter is best used to describe "intellectual" album-oriented rock by such British bands as Genesis, King Crimson, Pink Floyd, and Yes. The term "art rock" is best used to describe either classically influenced rock by such British groups as the Electric Light Orchestra (ELO), Emerson, Lake and Palmer (ELP), Gentle Giant, the Moody Blues, and Procol Harum or the fusion of progressive rock and English folk music created by such groups as Jethro Tull and the Strawbs. In common, all these bands regularly employ complicated and conceptual approaches to their music. Moreover, there has been a relatively fluid movement of musicians between bands that fall under the most general definition of art rock. Among the musicians who contributed to numerous bands are Bill Bruford (Yes, King Crimson, and U.K.), Steve Howe (Yes and Asia), Greg Lake (King Crimson and ELP), and John Wetton (King Crimson, U.K., and Asia). Some of the experimental rock by such American and

PERFORMANCE ARTIST LAURIE ANDERSON

Laurie Anderson, born June 5, 1947 in Wayne, Illinois, began studying classical violin, at five years of age and later performed with the Chicago Youth Symphony. In 1966 she moved to New York City, where she attended Barnard College (B.A., 1969) and Columbia University (M.F.A., 1972). For two years she taught art history at the City University of New York.

(*continued on the next page*)

Laurie Anderson performs at the Annual Cabaret for the American Academy in Rome, a charity event in New York City, on November 5, 2014.

(*continued from the previous page*)

One of Anderson's early performance art pieces was *Automotive* (1972), for which she orchestrated car horns at the Town Green in Rochester, Vermont. In *Duets on Ice*, another early piece, Anderson wore ice skates frozen in blocks of ice; she then proceeded to play a duet with herself on an altered violin that she described as like a "ventriloquist's dummy"— she replaced the bow hair with prerecorded audiotape and the strings with a tape head. The piece ended as soon as the ice melted.

To support her work in performance art, Anderson worked as a freelance interviewer and art critic for *ARTnews* and *Artforum*. By 1974 she had received several grants that gave her more freedom to pursue her artistic explorations. She came to rely on a driving rock beat as a backdrop to many of her word-oriented pieces; this led to a musical single, "It's Not the Bullet That Kills You—It's the Hole" (1977). Another song, the eight-minute "O Superman" (1981), reached the number two spot on England's pop charts. She released the recordings *You're the Guy I Want to Share My Money With* (1981), *Big Science* (1982), and *Mister Heartbreak* (1984) before producing a massive four-part multimedia extravaganza,

United States I–IV. It combined music, photography, film, drawings, and animation with text and consisted of 78 segments organized into four sections: Transportation, Politics, Money, and Love. First performed at the Brooklyn Academy of Music in 1983, it ran for more than six hours and employed more than 1,200 photos, cartoons, and films. She used some of the same material again in writing, directing, and performing in the film *Home of the Brave* (1986). Anderson's later recordings include *Strange Angels* (1989), *Bright Red* (1994), and *The Ugly One with the Jewels* and *Other Stories* (1995).

Anderson later served as NASA's artist-in-residence (2002–04), and the experience inspired her one-woman show *The End of the Moon,* which debuted in 2004. Her other projects include *The Waters Reglitterized* (2005), an installation inspired by her dreams, and the albums *Life on a String* (2001) and *Homeland* (2010). Anderson also collaborated on the opening ceremony for the 2004 Olympic Games in Athens.

Beginning in the mid-1990s, Anderson was in a relationship with musician Lou Reed; they were married from 2008 until his death in 2013.

British artists as Laurie Anderson, David Bowie, Brian Eno, the Velvet Underground, and Frank Zappa is also often categorized as art rock.

Art rock often featured complicated and frequent rhythm changes, imaginative lyrics (including sociopolitical or science-fiction themes), and unified, extended compositions (often in the form of "concept albums"). Classical instrumentation (including symphony orchestras) and pseudo-orchestral ensemble playing by rock bands (including reworkings of classical compositions) were also prevalent. Art rock had widespread appeal in its virtuosity and in the complexity of its music and lyrics, and it was intended primarily for listening and contemplation rather than for dancing.

SINGER-SONGWRITERS

From folk rock and the far-reaching influence of Bob Dylan grew the singer-songwriter movement of the 1970s. Preeminent singer-songwriters included Joni Mitchell, Van Morrison, Neil Young, Randy Newman, James Taylor, Carly Simon, Cat Stevens, Carole King, and Jackson Browne. Their music, while highly individualized, shared introspective, poetic, and often autobiographical lyrics sung in idiosyncratic voices.

Among the most successful artists to emerge from the singer-songwriter tradition was Bruce Springsteen. He began his career in the early 1970s, playing in East Coast cities and building a reputation as a charismatic stage performer. Pairing a rough-edged baritone voice with a classic rock sound, his most characteristic songs were insightful, sensitive portraits of working people. Springsteen continued recording and touring into the 2000s, sometimes with his E Street Band and sometimes with other musicians or as a solo artist.

DISCO

Discotheques, or nightclubs, offering recorded rock music for dancing, first appeared in the 1960s. In the 1970s long rock songs, usually played at fast tempos and with skipping rhythms, became known as disco music. Disco was strongly influenced by upbeat Motown songs, the syncopated rhythms of funk, and the sweet melodies of pop soul. Popular disco stars included Gloria Gaynor and Donna Summer. Disco music was featured in the movie *Saturday Night Fever*, and an album of music from the film, performed by the Bee Gees, became the most popular record of the 1970s. Although disco came under harsh criticism for its commerciality, the genre can be credited as the precursor to such later dance music styles as house and techno.

Madonna, one of the most successful pop stars of all time, began her career in the early 1980s with disco-inspired dance hits such as "Holiday." She had a keen eye and ear for translating trends from the underground club culture into pop songs. A former dancer herself, Madonna never strayed far from her roots in dance and club music. Her 1998 album *Ray of Light* brought techno music into the mainstream.

GLAM ROCK

A musical movement that began in Britain in the early 1970s, glam rock (also called glitter rock) brought over-the-top spectacle to the rock arena. The preeminent glam rocker was David Bowie. With the 1972 album *The Rise and Fall of Ziggy Stardust and The Spiders from Mars*, Bowie introduced the first of his several theatrical personae, Ziggy Stardust, a fey-looking alien rock star. Musically, the album was quintessential glam, combining aggressive guitar-oriented hard rock, foreboding lyrics, and catchy, pop-influenced choruses. Other British performers associated with glam rock included Queen, Roxy Music, and Elton John, who combined glam rock's showmanship with diverse pop musical styles. In the United States glam rock engendered such diverse musical acts as Lou Reed of the Velvet Underground, the early punk band the New York Dolls, and the hard-rocking and heavily made-up Kiss.

PUNK ROCK

Punk, which exploded on the American and British music scenes in the 1970s, was stripped-down hard-rock music paired with hostile lyrics typically condemning the consumerism of modern urban society. Punk also made a radical fashion statement—torn clothes, leather jackets, and garishly dyed hair, with razor blades and safety pins for decoration—to embody teen rebellion and alienation.

Punk found much to condemn in the British ruling class, and the British group the Sex Pistols, featuring Johnny Rotten and Sid Vicious, was the definitive punk band, offering such classic anthems as "Anarchy in the U.K." Another notable British punk band was the Clash. Bands that defined the American punk scene included Iggy and the Stooges, the Ramones, and the Patti Smith Group. Punk was largely eclipsed by disco in the late 1970s, but its spirit survived into the 1980s, albeit mostly underground, with the post-punk offshoots hardcore and new wave. The British band Joy Division, which later became New Order, was a notable success of the late punk era.

HEAVY METAL

The antecedents of heavy metal's signature drums, bass, and distorted electric guitar were the blues-based rock of mid-1960s British bands, the guitar virtuosity of Jimi Hendrix, and the stage shows of glam rock. The early 1970s pioneers of the genre included Led Zeppelin, Deep Purple, and Black Sabbath. Throughout the '70s metal bands such as Kiss, AC/DC, Aerosmith, Judas Priest, and Alice Cooper gained an international following mainly through extensive touring.

A new wave of British metal acts, including Def Leppard and Iron Maiden, along with the innovative guitar playing of Eddie Van Halen, revived the genre in the 1980s. Heavy metal achieved its greatest mainstream success in that decade with such pop-oriented bands as Mötley Crüe, Poison, Bon Jovi, and Guns N' Roses. In opposition to their commercialism, harder styles of metal arose, some of which flourished underground. Metallica, Megadeth, Anthrax, and Slayer were among the bands that pioneered thrash metal, characterized by a fast tempo and aggressive lyrics.

NEW WAVE

Taking its name from the French New Wave cinema of the 1950s, the new wave genre of popular music arose in the late 1970s. It fused an arty sensibility with the do-it-yourself principle of punk to produce catchy and often subversively humorous music.

A diverse category, new wave encompassed such American artists as the

B-52s, Blondie, the Go-Go's, and the Cars. New wave innovators included Devo and Talking Heads, both composed of former art students. Among British new-wave acts were the clever singer-songwriters Elvis Costello and Nick Lowe; Squeeze and XTC, whose songs were sophisticated and infectious; and the so-called New Romantics, including Duran Duran and Adam and the Ants. By the mid-1980s the distinction between new wave and mainstream "corporate" rock was blurred, especially for such commercially successful bands as the Pretenders, the Police, and U2. New wave's impact on pop music continued through the 1990s.

ALTERNATIVE AND INDIE ROCK

By the mid-1980s rock, then three decades old, had evolved from its controversial origins into a well-established part of popular culture. No longer an expression of youthful rebellion, rock had become mainstream music predominantly for adults. In reaction against conventional rock, some independent-minded bands of the 1980s and 1990s sought to stretch the rock tradition to create something newly personal. Their music was labeled alternative rock. R.E.M., the quintessential college-radio stars of the 1980s, was the most successful of early alternative rock bands.

The breakthrough moment for alternative rock was the 1991 release of the single "Smells Like Teen Spirit" by the band Nirvana. Inspired by the aggression of punk and heavy metal, the music of Nirvana featured distorted guitars and ravaged vocals expressing alienation, anger, and despair. With the success of local bands Nirvana and Pearl Jam, Seattle, Washington, became ground zero for a new musical style called grunge. While the popularity of grunge faded in the mid-1990s, its lasting influence was bringing alternative rock to the mainstream audience.

Another term that came to be applied to alternative rock bands was "indie rock." "Indie" was short for "independent," referring to the fact that many of the bands released their music through independent record labels rather than the major labels. Eventually "indie" came to identify the genre more than the method of distribution. In the 21st century "indie rock" remained a sort of catch-all term for idiosyncratic artists working outside of the mainstream.

THE ONGOING EVOLUTION OF ROCK

This overview of the music's evolution over the decades shows how rock became the most inclusive of musical labels. It encompassed a broad range of sounds and styles, many of which bore little resemblance to the original rock and roll of the 1950s. The defining quality that unified these diverse sounds under the label of rock was authenticity. Rock was distinguished from pop music in that the main motivation of its makers was not commercial sales but rather the authentic expression of the songwriter's or performer's feelings or worldview. Rock, then, was defined more by an attitude than by any particular sound.

With authenticity as the leading criterion, rock in the 21st century continued to embrace a great variety of artists. One measure of this diversity was the lineups at rock festivals staged throughout the United States, Europe, and other parts of the world. Hip-hop stars such as Jay-Z and Kanye West played headlining sets alongside electronic/dance performers such as LCD Soundsystem and Daft Punk, art rock bands such as Radiohead and Arcade Fire, and "classic rock" acts such as Bruce Springsteen and Paul McCartney.

RAP MUSIC AND HIP-HOP

In the early 1970s Jamaican deejay Clive Campbell—known as Kool Herc—moved to the Bronx in New York City and introduced the innovations that developed into rap music. Using two turntables, he manipulated records to create longer dance segments while shouting out comments to the dancers during the instrumental breaks. Soon urban deejays began to team with so-called rappers, and the shouts developed into rhyming, rhythmic patter that was spoken or chanted over the percussive backing music, which came to be known as hip-hop. For years a popular technique of club deejays such as Herc and Afrika Bambaataa, rap produced its first hit song in 1979 with the Sugarhill Gang's "Rapper's Delight."

Following in the geographic (South Bronx) path of rap, the cultural movement known as hip-hop emerged in the late 1970s. Although music is a central component of hip-hop, it is also a complex culture that includes graffiti painting, a shared outlook, and an attitude known as B-boying. Dance is also key. Hip-hop partygoers developed an improvisational, acrobatic style of dancing called break dancing. The dancers came to be called "break boys" and "break girls," or "B-boys" and "B-girls" for short.

Originally confined to predominantly black neighborhoods in New York City, rap and hip-hop broke into the mainstream in the 1980s with the popularity of such performers as LL Cool J, Run-D.M.C., M.C. Hammer, and Will Smith. They kept the genre open and upbeat, moving toward the so-called "alternative" rap of De La Soul, the Fugees, TLC, and others whose work was made accessible to wide audiences through the fusion of rap, pop, and soul music. Lauryn Hill, a member of the Fugees, dominated the 1999 Grammy Awards, winning five trophies for her solo album *The Miseducation of Lauryn Hill.*

Other rap acts used their music to take advantage of the political power of the spoken word. Among the earliest performers to make an overtly political statement was Grandmaster Flash and the Furious Five. Their groundbreaking song "The Message" (1982) opened the door for the angry militant rap of Public Enemy, who recorded the landmark albums *It Takes a Nation of Millions to Hold Us Back* (1988) and *Fear of a Black Planet* (1990). Public Enemy blurred the line between music and politics, using rap to speak directly of the rebellious mood of the disenfranchised. De La Soul offered densely layered samples and socially conscious lyrics on its influential debut album *3 Feet High and Rising* (1989). Formed in 1981, the Beastie Boys, blending hip-hop and rap, were the first white performers to gain a substantial following. As such, they were largely responsible for the growth of the forms' mainstream audience.

The West Coast group N.W.A. (Niggaz with Attitude), founded in 1986, popularized so-called gangsta ("gangster") rap, which graphically depicted (and some say glorified) violence and drug dealing. In the 1990s gangsta rap became the genre's dominant style, making stars of such acts as Snoop Doggy Dogg (later called Snoop Dogg and Snoop Lion), Ice-T, and Tupac

Shakur (2Pac). The violence chronicled in their songs spilled over into real life in 1996–97 with the shocking murders of Shakur and another popular performer known as the Notorious B.I.G.

As rap evolved, it saw greater diversification of voices and geographical centers. Female rappers, such as Queen Latifah and Salt-n-Pepa, provided an alternative to rap's predominantly male viewpoint. Notable artists outside of New York City included DJ Jazzy Jeff and the Fresh Prince (Will Smith) from Philadelphia, who starred in their own television sitcom; 2 Live Crew from Miami, Florida, whose album *As Nasty as They Wanna Be* (1989) was banned as obscene for its provocative lyrics; and M.C. Hammer from Oakland, California, who achieved massive but short-lived success with the album *Please Hammer Don't Hurt 'Em* (1990).

Foremost among the rappers who achieved superstardom in the late 1990s and early 2000s were Eminem, Jay-Z, and Kanye West. With Dr. Dre, formerly of N.W.A., as his producer and mentor, Eminem reached multiplatinum sales with the albums *The Slim Shady LP* (1999) and *The Marshall Mathers LP* (2000). He also drew much criticism for the treatment of women and gays in his lyrics.

Beginning with *Reasonable Doubt* in 1996, Jay-Z released a series of successful albums before becoming president of the influential

Def Jam record label and expanding into a number of other business ventures. Kanye West, one of Jay-Z's producers, emerged as one of the most fascinating characters in rap following the success of his 2004 debut album *The College Dropout.* With his innovative music and deeply personal lyrics, West opened up the possibilities of rap and greatly influenced the artistic direction of the genre.

In the late 1990s hip-hop became the best-selling genre of popular music in the United States and also a global phenomenon. Popular rap artists of the time included the Wu-Tang Clan and Diddy (known by a variety of names, including Sean "Puffy" Combs and Puff Daddy), performer, producer, and president of Bad Boy Records.

Beginning in the late 20th century, many of the most popular rappers came from the American South. The duo OutKast emerged from Atlanta in the 1990s and scored huge crossover successes in the 2000s with *Stankonia* (2000) and *Speakerboxxx/The Love Below* (2003). Other stars who rose from the South included Ludacris and T.I., also from Atlanta, and Lil Wayne, from New Orleans.

In the early 21st century hip-hop continues to move into the mainstream and remains a dominant force on the pop music charts. Perhaps no one has represented the cultural triumph of hip-hop better than Jay-Z.

As his career has progressed, he went from performing artist to label president, head of a clothing line, club owner, and market consultant. Along the way he broke Elvis Presley's *Billboard* magazine record for the most number one albums by a solo artist.

Beyoncé and Jay-Z get down onstage for the 56th Grammy Awards at the Staples Center in Los Angeles, on Jan. 26, 2014.

the consciousness of consumers the idea of downloading songs from the Internet—bypassing the purchase of established distribution forms, such as records, tapes, or CDs. Then of course there are such sites as iTunes, Spotify, Pandora, SoundCloud, and Hype Machine.

You never know what's coming next with music. Or what's coming back. Take vinyl records, a relic from the late 20th century. Dead in the water, right? Not so much. While still only a fraction of total music sales, since around 2000, vinyl sales—sometimes referred to as the vinyl revival—have surged. Mix tapes have come back, too, albeit in another form: playlists.

Want to predict what happens next? Good luck. It's a long and winding road. And it ain't over 'til the fat lady sings.

GLOSSARY

air de cour Genre of French solo or part-song predominant from the late 16th century through the 17th century. It originated in arrangements, for voice and lute, of popular chansons written in a light chordal style.

aleatory Also called chance music (aleatory from Latin *alea*, "dice"), 20th-century music in which chance or indeterminate elements are left for the performer to realize.

aural Of or relating to the ear or to the sense of hearing.

ballade One of several *formes fixes* ("fixed forms") in French lyric poetry and song, cultivated particularly in the 14th and 15th centuries. Strictly, the ballade consists of three stanzas and a shortened final dedicatory stanza.

cantata Large work for a chorus of singers and accompanying instruments.

discordant Describes a combination of musical sounds that strike the ear harshly.

idiomatic Describes an expression that cannot be understood from the meanings of its separate words but must be learned as a whole; the expression "give way," meaning "retreat," is an idiom

improvisation The act of composing, reciting, playing, or singing on the spur of the moment or without planning.

madrigal Complex polyphonic unaccompanied vocal piece on a secular text developed especially in the 16th and 17th centuries.

mass Series of prayers and ceremonies forming the eucharistic (communion) service, especially of the Roman Catholic Church.

microphone Instrument whereby sound waves are caused to generate or modulate an electric current usually for the purpose of transmitting or recording sound (as speech or music).

motet Polyphonic choral composition on a sacred text usually without instrumental accompaniment.

oratorio Large-scale musical composition for solo voices, chorus, and orchestra using a sacred or semi-sacred text.

pedagogical Of or relating to teaching or educating.

polyphonic Of or relating to a style of musical composition employing two or more simultaneous but relatively independent melodic lines.

qin Fretless Chinese board zither with seven strings.

rhythm Flow of sound in music having regular accented beats.

rondeau Fixed form of verse based on two rhyme sounds and consisting usually of 13 lines in three stanzas with the opening words of the first line of the first stanza used as an independent refrain after the second and third stanzas.

tantara The blare of a trumpet or horn.

tempo Rate of speed at which a musical piece or passage is to be played or sung.

transistor radio Radio developed in the 1950s that has transistors, a transistor being an electronic device consisting of a small block of a semiconductor (as germanium) with at least three electrodes and that is used to control the flow of electricity in electronic equipment (such as a radio or a computer).

troubadour One of a class of lyric poets and poet-musicians often of knightly rank who flourished from the 11th to the end of the 13th century chiefly in the south of France and the north of Italy and whose major theme was courtly love.

trouvère One of a school of poets who flourished from the 11th to the 14th centuries and who composed mostly narrative works.

BIBLIOGRAPHY

MODERN THEORIES OF MUSICAL MEANING

Arthur Schopenhauer, *Die Welt als Wille und Vorstellung* (1883; Eng. trans., *The World as Will and Idea*, 1961); and Friedrich Nietzsche, "The Birth of Tragedy from the Spirit of Music," trans. by Clifton P. Fadiman in *The Philosophy of Nietzsche* (1954), are two important expositions. Eduard Hanslick, *Vom musikalisch Schönen* (1854; Eng. trans., *The Beautiful in Music*, 1957), remains the best single exposition of the formalist (or nonreferentialist) position in musical aesthetics. Edmund Gurney, *The Power of Sound* (1880, reprinted 1966), maintains a similar point of view but with considerably greater amplitude and subtlety. For background of the contemporary symbolist views of musical meaning, see Alfred North Whitehead, *Symbolism* (1959); Susanne K. Langer, "On Significance in Music," in *Philosophy in a New Key,* 2nd ed. (1951), and *Feeling and Form* (1953). Leonard B. Meyer has made an important contribution to the aesthetics of music. His interest in the relevance of information theory to music has been evidenced in two articles: "Meaning in Music and Information Theory," *Journal of Aesthetics and Art Criticism*, 14:412–424 (1957), and "Some Remarks on Value and Greatness in Music," ibid., 17:486–500 (1959), reprinted in his *Music, The Arts, and Ideas: Patterns and Predictions in Twentieth-Century Culture* (1967). Also see his *Style and Music* (1989). John Dewey, *Art as Experience* (1934, reprinted 1959); and Karl Jaspers, *Von der Wahrheit* (1947; Eng. trans., *Truth and Symbol*, 1959), have given reinforcement to organic and symbolic theses, respectively. Peter Le Huray and James Day (eds.), *Music and Aesthetics in the Eighteenth and Early-Nineteenth Centuries* (1981), expounds theories of musical aesthetics from the pre- and early-Romantic period. Peter Kivy, *The Corded Shell* (1981), is a study of the emotional expressivity of music. Newer general sources include Nicholas Cook, *Music: A Very Short Introduction* (2000), Richard Taruskin, *A History of Western Music* (2004), Lawrence Ferrara. *Philosophy and the Analysis of Music* (1991), and *Music in the Twentieth and Twenty-First Centuries*, by Joseph Auner (2013).

PERFORMANCE PRACTICE, STYLES, AND MUSICAL FORMS

The best historical accounts of musical forms, styles, and performance practice are to be found in Donald J. Grout, *A History of*

Western Music (1960); Gustave Reese, *Music in the Middle Ages* (1940), and *Music in the Renaissance*, rev. ed. (1959); Manfred F. Bukofzer, *Music in the Baroque Era* (1947); Alfred Einstein, *Music in the Romantic Era* (1947); and William W. Austin, *Music in the 20th Century, from Debussy to Stravinsky* (1966). Sir Donald Francis Tovey, *The Forms of Music* (1956), contains informative and engaging short pieces. Robert Schumann, *On Music and Musicians*, ed. by Konrad Wolff (Eng. trans. 1947), is an example of the work by a 19th-century precursor of the phenomenon of the present-day composer-authors who have contributed to aesthetic theory by elucidating their own works and commentating on other composers and on the scene in general. See also Igor Stravinsky, *Poetics of Music in the Form of Six Lessons* (1947); Paul Hindemith, *A Composer's World* (1952); Aaron Copland, *Music and Imagination* (1952). Discussion of music and film may be found in Lewis Jacobs (ed.), *The Emergence of Film Art* (1969). Twelve-tone technique and varieties of serialism deriving from it are treated in Arnold Schoenberg, *Style and Idea* (1950); and René Leibowitz, *Schoenberg, et son école* (1947; Eng. trans., *Schoenberg and His School*, 1949). Short pieces on electronic music appear often in periodical literature. Harold C. Schonberg, *Facing the Music* (1981), is a collection of performance-oriented articles. See also Carol MacClintock (ed.), *Readings in the History of Music in Performance* (1979). Also recommended are Wallace Berry. *Musical Structure and Performance* (1989) and *Classical and Romantic Performing Practice 1750-1900*, by Clive Brown (1999).

CHINESE MUSIC

Western-language sources are listed in Fredric Lieberman, *Chinese Music: An Annotated Bibliography*, 2nd, rev. and enlarged ed. (1979). Also of interest are Rulan Chao Pian, *Song Dynasty Musical Sources and Their Interpretation* (1967); R.H. van Gulik, *The Lore of the Chinese Lute*, new ed., rev. (1969); Laurence Picken (ed.), *Music from the Tang Court*, 5 vol. (1981–90); Kenneth J. DeWoskin, *A Song for One or Two: Music and the Concept of Art in Early China* (1982); Liang Mingyue (Ming-yüen Liang), *Music of the Billion: An Introduction to Chinese Musical Culture* (1985); Bell Yung, *Cantonese Opera* (1989).

VOCAL MUSIC

K. E. Miller, (1988). Vocal Music Education
Daniel Moe. *Basic Choral Concepts* (1972).
B. J.Monahan, *The Art of Singing* (1978). Ray
Robinson, ed. *Choral Music: Norton Historical
Anthology* (1978). Homer Ulrich. *A Survey of
Choral Music* (1973).

MUSICAL RECORDING

Roland Gelatt, *The Fabulous Phonograph*,
2nd rev. ed. (1977), a general history of
the phonograph, particularly good on the
complex corporate developments; Oliver
Read and Walter L. Welch, *From Tin Foil to
Stereo*, 2nd ed. (1976), a scholarly and
detailed phonographic history with much
elucidation of technical matters; Frederic W.
Wile, *Emile Berliner: Maker of the Microphone*
(1926, reprinted 1974), an adulatory, but
worthwhile, biography; Fred Gaisberg, *The
Music Goes Round* (1942, reprinted 1977), an
autobiographical account of the history of
the phonograph by a man associated with
Berliner from the earliest days (a valuable
source despite many inaccuracies); Matthew
Josephson, *Edison* (1959), a thoroughly

researched biography of the inventor of the phonograph; Joseph Batten, *Joe Batten's Book: The Story of Sound Recording* (1956), another personal documentation of early phonographic history, not as far-ranging as Gaisberg's but with much unduplicated material. Russell Miller and Roger Boar, *The Incredible Music Machine* (1982), is a popular history. Another robust source is *Early Recordings and Musical Style: Changing Tastes in Instrumental Performance*, 1900–1950 by Robert Philip (1992; 2004).

CLASSICAL MUSIC

Denis Arnold. *The New Oxford Companion to Music*, 2 vols (1983). Michael Kennedy. *Oxford Dictionary of Music* (1985). Brian Morton and Pamela Collins, (eds). *Contemporary Composers* (1992). Stanley Sadie, (ed). *The New Grove Dictionary of Music and Musicians*, 20 vols. (1980). Nicolas Slonimsky. *Music Since 1900*, 4th ed.; *Supplement* (1971; 1986). Nicolas Slonimsky, (ed). *Baker's Biographical Dictionary of Musicians*, 7th rev. (ed). (1984). Charles Rosen. *The Classical Style*. (Expanded Edition). (1997), D.

Schulenberg, *Music of the Baroque.* (2007).
William E. Caplin, *Classical Form: A Theory of
Formal Functions for the Instrumental Music
of Haydn, Mozart, and Beethoven* (1998).

JAZZ

Joachim Berendt. *The Jazz Book,* rev. (ed).
(1982). Ian Carr and others. *Jazz: The
Essential Companion* (1988). J. L. Collier. *The
Making of Jazz* (1979). Linda Dahl. *Stormy
Weather: The Music and Lives of a Century
of Jazzwomen* (1989). Leonard Feather. *The
Encyclopedia of Jazz* (1984). Ira Gitler. *Jazz
Masters of the Forties* (1982). M. C. Gridley.
Jazz Styles, 3rd ed. (1987). Richard Hadlock.
Jazz Masters of the Twenties (1986). John
Litweiler. *The Freedom Principle* (1989).
Nat Shapiro and Nat Hentoff, (eds). *Hear
Me Talkin' to Ya* (1966). Studs Terkel. *Giants
of Jazz,* rev. ed. (1975). Valerie Wilmer. *As
Serious as Your Life* (1980). G. Schuller. *Early
Jazz: Its Roots and Musical Development of
Jazz* (1989). G. Schuller, *The Swing Era: The
Development of Jazz,* 1930-1945.

ROCK MUSIC

GENERAL

There is an extensive literature on rock that ranges from academic musicology and sociology through every kind of journalism to disposable gossip and poster books. Peter van der Merwe, *Origins of the Popular Style* (1989, reissued 1992), a scholarly study of pre-20th-century popular music, helps explain why a music first appearing at the margins of Western culture so quickly became the mainstream. *Charlie Gillett, The Sound of the City: The Rise of Rock and Roll*, 2nd ed., newly illustrated and expanded (1996), is still the best account of how rock and roll was first shaped in a variety of local American settings. Rock and roll's roots in black and white music are covered in *Country: The Music and the Musicians: From the Beginnings to the '90s*, 2nd ed. (1994), an informative overview of country music history published by the Country Music Foundation; and Charles Keil, *Urban Blues* (1966, reissued 1991), an illuminating anthropological study of black American musical culture in the late 1950s and early 1960s. Tim J. Anderson, *Making Easy Listening: Material Culture and Postwar American Recording* (2006), is a valuable overview of the changes in the American recording industry that made new ways of music making and listening possible.

The development of rock out of rock and roll was as much an ideological as a musical process, and the classic description of that ideology—of why and how rock drew from and came to articulate the contradictory impulses of American popular culture—is Greil Marcus, *Mystery Train*, 4th rev. ed. (1997), which, in its studies of particular musicians, was the first work to reveal the possibilities of rock criticism; Greil Marcus, *Invisible Republic: Bob Dylan's Basement Tapes* (1997), fills the biggest gap in *Mystery Train*. Simon Frith and Howard Horne, *Art into Pop* (1987), studies how British rock sensibility was shaped by art school ideas and practices. Theodore Gracyk, *Listening to Popular Music; or, How I Learned to Stop Worrying and Love Led Zeppelin* (2007), is an illuminating philosophical investigation of rock fans' values.

Simon Frith and Andrew Goodwin (eds.), *On Record: Rock, Pop, and the Written Word* (1990), is a useful anthology of 30 years of scholarly writing on rock, from a variety of disciplinary perspectives. The best studies of the rock music industry are Geoffrey Stokes, *Star-Making Machinery* (1976), a fine and undated piece of reportage on the making and marketing of a Commander Cody LP; Andrew Goodwin, *Dancing in the Distraction Factory: Music Television and Popular Culture*

(1992), a lucid and thoughtful analysis of MTV's impact on rock culture; and Paul Théberge, *Any Sound You Can Imagine: Making Music/Consuming Technology* (1997), a comprehensive history of the effects of technology on music making, paying particular attention to digital technology. Kembrew McLeod, *Freedom of Expression®: Overzealous Copyright Bozos and Other Enemies of Creativity* (2005), is a polemic on the copyright wars of the early 21st century that captures something of rock's DIY spirit.

BIOGRAPHIES

Elvis Presley is the focus of Peter Guralnick, *Last Train to Memphis* (1994), the definitive work on the young Presley and his influences, and *Careless Love* (1999), providing all one needs to know about Presley's subsequent career—its triumphs and tragedies. Good accounts of the ways in which musicians have tried to make sense of rock's confusion of art, commerce, and politics can be found in the biographies of four musicians who died young: Marc Eliot, *Death of a Rebel* (1979, reissued 1995), on the muddled life of folk-rock singer-songwriter Phil Ochs; Charles Shaar Murray, *Crosstown Traffic* (1989), a biography of Jimi Hendrix focusing on issues of race and identity; Dr.

Licks, *Standing in the Shadows of Motown: The Life and Music of Legendary Bassist James Jamerson* (1989), a loving account of the origins and influence of one of rock's most significant rhythmic stylists; and Armond White, *Rebel for the Hell of It* (1997), on rap star Tupac (2Pac) Shakur, an important reflection on music and the state of the American nation at the end of the 20th century. Bob Dylan, *Chronicles* (2004), the first volume of his biography, is necessary reading for anyone wanting to understand that rock is indeed part of the centuries-long story of American popular music; while Joe Boyd, *White Bicycles: Making Music in the 1960s* (2006), is an invaluable memoir of someone who was at the centre of all the musical, geographical, and commercial crosscurrents that drove the development of rock since its golden age.

GENRES

The most-enlightening books on particular musical genres are Andrew Holleran, *Dancer from the Dance* (1978, reissued 1990), a novel that captures the disco experience better than any other writing; Dick Hebdige, *Cut 'n' Mix: Culture, Identity, and Caribbean Music* (1987, reissued 1990), a suggestive application of cultural theory to the remarkable mobility of reggae music; Jon Savage, *England's Dreaming: Sex Pistols and Punk Rock* (1991; also published as *England's Dreaming: Anarchy, Sex Pistols, Punk Rock, and Beyond,* 1992), on music, suburbia, and boredom; David Toop, *Rap Attack 2: African Rap to Global Hip Hop,* rev. ed. (1991), a well-informed history of early hip-hop; Joseph G. Schloss, *Making Beats: The Art of Sample-Based Hip-Hop* (2004), takes the story forward; Robert Walser, *Running with the Devil: Power, Gender, and Madness in Heavy Metal Music* (1993), the most convincing of all the musicological rock studies; Sarah Thornton, *Club Cultures: Music, Media, and Subcultural Capital* (1995), an intelligent sociology of British dance clubs in the early 1990s; and Simon Reynolds, *Generation Ecstasy: Into the World of Techno and Rave Culture* (1998), and *Rip It Up and Start Again: Postpunk 1978–1984* (2006), are helpful maps of a confused music scene. Finally, Evelyn McDonnell and Ann Powers (eds.), *Rock She Wrote* (1995), is an instructive anthology of rock writing from a female perspective; Mark Slobin, *Subcultural Sounds: Micromusics of the West* (1993), is an ethnomusicological study which makes clear that all popular musics, rock included, remain local even as they become global, just as in the first days of rock and roll; and

Shane Homan, *Access All Eras: Tribute Bands and Global Pop Culture* (2006), provides an amusing take on the global phenomenon of rock nostalgia.

ART ROCK

Edward Macan, *Rocking the Classics: English Progressive Rock and the Counterculture* (1997), a comprehensive work, discusses the origin of progressive rock; its musical, visual, and lyrical styles; and its critical reception. Bill Martin, *Music of Yes: Structure and Vision in Progressive Rock* (1996), treats Yes's early music, 1970s albums, band members' solo projects, and later manifestations of the band; to a certain extent, the work applies sociocultural theory to Yes by focusing on individual works by the group. Eric Tamm, *Brian Eno: His Music and the Vertical Color of Sound*, updated ed. (1995), systematically accounts for Eno's musical compositions and other activities, including his progressive rock from the mid-1970s, his later ambient style, his collaborations as a cocomposer and producer, and his views on cultural aesthetics; and Tamm's *Robert Fripp: From King Crimson to Guitar Craft* (1990), treats Fripp as a progressive-rock guitarist before, during, and in between his several incarnations of the band King Crimson, his collaborations as a guitarist and producer, his experimental developments of "Frippertronics" and other forms, and his later activities as a music theorist and teacher.

HIP-HOP

David Toop, *Rap Attack 3: African Rap to Global Hip Hop* (1999), is probably the book most successful at revealing hip-hop's debts to earlier forms of black American popular music. In answer to the question of whether hip-hop lyrics are a form of poetry, Lawrence A. Stanley (ed.), *Rap: The Lyrics* (1992), allows readers to make up their own minds by presenting the writings of hip-hop's greatest lyricists. Tricia Rose, *Black Noise: Rap Music and Black Culture in Contemporary America* (1994), argues that technology, urban sociology, race politics, and feminism have intersected in hip-hop to foment a hotbed of postmodern artistry and controversy. Nelson George, *Hip Hop America* (1998), presents a serious fan's view of the long road hip-hop took from street fests to mainstream market profitability and semirespectability. Havelock Nelson and Michael A. Gonzales, *Bring the Noise: A Guide to Rap Music and Hip-Hop*

Culture (1991), is a detailed introduction to the history of rap and a guide to the best recordings. Alan Light (ed.), *The Vibe History of Hip Hop* (1999), explores the full scope of hip-hop's origins and expansion with contributions from more than 50 writers; Jeff Chang, *Can't Stop, Won't Stop: A History of the Hip-Hop Generation* (2005), examines the sociocultural and musical history of the genre; Murray Forman and Mark Anthony Neal (eds.), *That's the Joint!: The Hip-Hop Studies Reader* (2004), is a wide-ranging anthology of writings from both the academic and popular press; Sacha Jenkins, Elliott Wilson, Chairman Mao, Gabriel Alvarez, and Brent Rollins, *Ego Trip's Book of Rap Lists* (1999), is humorous and opinionated but dense with information and true to the spirit of the culture.

INDEX